Editors
Erica N. Russikoff, M.A.
Andrea Tropeano, M.A.

Illustrator
Clint McKnight

Cover Artists
Kevin Barnes
Barb Lorseyedi

Editor in Chief
Ina Massler Levin, M.A.

Creative Director
Karen J. Goldfluss, M.S. Ed.

Art Coordinator
Renée Christine Yates

Imaging
Rosa C. See

Publisher
Mary D. Smith, M.S. Ed.

Author

Garth Sundem, M.M.

Teacher Created Resources, Inc.
6421 Industry Way
Westminster, CA 92683
www.teachercreated.com

ISBN: 978-1-4206-2565-3

© 2009 Teacher Created Resources, Inc.
Made in U.S.A.

Table of Contents

Introduction 4
Puzzle Hints 5–6

Picture Puzzles 7–28
Shape Find 7
Fit It! 7
Solid Gold Game 8
Shape Construction 9
What's Different? 9
Ad Match 10
Triangle Take-Away
  Game 11
Map Madness! 12
Split Shapes 13
Rebus 13
Shape Slap 14
Split Shapes 15
Fit It! 15
Shape Construction 16
What's Different? 16
Tangram Game 17
Map Madness! 18
Rebus 19
Shape Find 19
What's Different? 19
Cartoon Helpers 20
Split Shapes 21
Fit It! 21
Shape Construction 22
Shape Find 22
Rebus 22
Split Shapes 23
Solid Gold Game 23
Rebus 24
What's Different? 24
Shape Slap 25
Map Madness! 26
Fit It! 27

Rebus 27
Triangle Take-Away
  Game 28

Word Puzzles 29–52
Transformers 29
Missing Letter 29
Crossword 29
Hide and Seek 30
Crack the Code 30
Letter Scramble 30
Before and After 30
Rhyme Game 31
Hide and Seek 32
Crack the Code 32
Transformers 32
Letter Scramble 33
Transformers 33
Missing Letter 33
Crossword Challenge 34
Letter Scramble 35
Crossword 35
Before and After 35
Crack the Code 36
Hide and Seek 36
Letter Scramble 36
Before and After 36
Beginnings and
  Ends Game 37
Hide and Seek 38
Crossword 38
Missing Letter 38
Before and After 39
Letter Scramble 39
Hide and Seek 39
Crack the Code 39

Changing Letters 40
Hide and Seek 41
Missing Letter 41
Transformers 41
Crossword 42
Letter Scramble 42
Before and After 42
Fronts and Backs 43
Crack the Code 44
Hide and Seek 44
Transformers 44
Before and After 45
Crossword 45
Missing Letter 45
Crossword Challenge 46
Hide and Seek 47
Letter Scramble 47
Crack the Code 47
Missing Letter 47
Transformers 48
Letter Scramble 48
Crossword 48
Changing Letters 49
Letter Scramble 50
Missing Letter 50
Hide and Seek 50
Before and After 50
Transformers 51
Letter Scramble 51
Crossword 51
Letter Scramble 52
Hide and Seek 52
Letter Scramble 52
Before and After 52

Table of Contents *(cont.)*

Number Puzzles 53–79

Sudoku 53

In Addition 53

Addition Tree 54

It's Touching 54

Snake Race 55

Math Path 56

Sudoku 56

Fill in the Blanks. 57

Thinking of a Number 57

In Addition 57

Tic-Tac-Toe Race 58

Sudoku 59

In Addition 59

Fill in the Blanks. 60

Math Path 60

It's Touching 60

Meet Your Match 61

Sudoku 62

Thinking of a Number 62

Addition Tree 62

Fill in the Blanks. 63

Math Path 63

In Addition 63

Plus or Minus Game 64

Thinking of a Number 65

It's Touching 65

Sudoku 65

In Addition 66

Addition Tree 66

Addition Challenge. 67

Fill in the Blanks. 68

Sudoku 68

In Addition 68

It's Touching 69

Thinking of a Number 69

Math Path 69

Snake Race 70

Sudoku 71

Addition Tree 71

Fill in the Blanks. 72

Thinking of a Number 72

In Addition 72

Addition Challenge. 73

It's Touching 74

Sudoku 74

Thinking of a Number 75

Math Path 75

In Addition 75

Operations Game 76

Sudoku 77

In Addition 77

Thinking of a Number 78

Fill in the Blanks. 78

Addition Tree 78

Sudoku Challenge. 79

Logic Puzzles 80–99

Mike, Anne, Fred,
   and Kate 80

How Old? 80

Add One or Two 81

What's Next?. 82

Kara's Kitten. 82

Four-in-a-Row. 83

Letter Box 84

How Old? 84

Odd Animal Out 84

Pipe Layer 85

Letter Box 86

Mike, Anne, Fred,
   Kate, and Tom. 86

Reversi 87

What's Next?. 88

Alice's Book 88

Blocked 89

Odd Animal Out 90

Mike, Anne, Fred,
   Kate, and Tom. 90

Boxed Out. 91

What's Next?. 92

Tanya's Balloon 92

Ship Shapes. 93

Letter Box 94

Mike, Anne, and Fred 94

Four-in-a-Line. 95

What's Next?. 96

How Old? 96

Odd Animal Out 96

Sprouts 97

Mike, Anne, Fred,
   and Kate 98

Letter Box 99

How Old? 99

Odd Animal Out 99

Answer Key 100–112

Introduction

Welcome to *Puzzles and Games That Make Kids Think*. This book contains 190 puzzles and games of more than 30 different types, each of which is not only fun, but also asks students to use their minds to figure out the solution. (There are no "word finds" here!) Students will find some of these puzzles difficult, while other puzzles will be easy. Some puzzles will take seconds, while others might take half an hour. All of the puzzles are a workout for the brain! Here are a few reasons why we think you will enjoy this book:

- Puzzle-based brain workouts create results. Research shows that a regimen of brainteasers can lead to higher scores on problem-solving tests.[1] Research also shows that using puzzles in the classroom can lead to increased student interest and involvement.[2]

- There are four categories of brainteasers in this book: picture, word, number, and logic, with puzzles (for individual students) and games (for pairs) for each category. Within each section, students will use diverse thinking skills—in a picture puzzle, students may draw lines on a geometric figure, and in a number puzzle, they may need to read complex directions. The wide variety of puzzles keeps students engaged and entertained.

- Each page of this book includes all of the needed directions and materials (other than writing utensils!), making it easy to distribute these puzzles to early finishers. Or, you may choose to copy and distribute puzzles as part of a reward system or weekly brain-buster challenge. Students will look forward to these fun puzzles, and you can rest assured that your classroom time will be spent productively. Another use of these puzzles is to spice up homework packets—strategically insert a puzzle or two to keep things lively!

- With a less experienced class, you may need to preview puzzle directions ahead of time (especially the two-person games and logic puzzles). Consider exploring the directions as a class before independent work time. Or, explain that reading and understanding the instructions is the first part of the puzzle! Because puzzle types repeat, students will gain more confidence in their ability to solve the puzzles as they spend more time with this book.

Be careful—these puzzles are addictive, and you can easily find yourself whiling away a prep period with pencil in hand!

[1] Howard, P. J. (1994). *The Owner's Manual for the Brain*. Charlotte, NC: Leornian Press.
[2] Finke, R. A., et al. (1992). *Creative Cognition: Theory, Research, and Applications*. Cambridge, MA: The MIT Press.

Puzzle Hints

Game Hints

Some games require the ability to read and understand somewhat tricky directions. Consider previewing directions with students beforehand. Also notice that some games require photocopying the book page (or allowing students to cut shapes or game boards from the book). With less experienced classes, you might play a full-class version of a game (teacher versus students) before allowing pairs to work independently. In hopes of keeping game directions brief and student friendly, many of the more intuitive directions have been omitted. If students have questions about game mechanics, encourage them to use their common sense.

Picture Puzzles

- *Fit It!:* If you like, trace (or copy) and cut out the shapes.

- *Map Madness!:* Make sure you start at the correct point. Then, follow the route with your finger. Remember, left or right depends on which way you are traveling!

- *Rebus:* Where are words and/or pictures in relation to each other or to other elements? Say these relationships aloud and listen for common phrases.

- *Shape Construction:* If you like, trace (or copy) and cut out the shapes.

- *Shape Find:* First, imagine the shape in your mind. Then, try to work around the figure systematically. And don't forget the whole figure itself!

- *Shape Slap:* Use the big shapes first. Place them in ways that will block your opponent.

- *Split Shapes:* Usually the lines are drawn from corners. Start there first.

- *What's Different?:* Pretend there is a grid over each picture, and confine your search to only one box at a time.

Word Puzzles

- *Before and After:* If it doesn't come to you right away, brainstorm words that would fit the correct number of boxes.

- *Crack the Code:* Fill in each box in order. If you're running out of time, you can usually guess the answer before finishing the last few boxes.

- *Crossword:* Do the easy ones first. Then, use those letters to help you determine the more difficult ones.

- *Crossword Challenge:* The only way to do this is to guess and check. Start by adding the first word wherever you can, and then try to make the rest fit. Write lightly in pencil in case you have to erase the words and start again!

- *Hide and Seek:* Scan the sentence slowly, looking for the names of different animals.

- *Letter Scramble:* Play with the vowel—it's usually the key.

- *Missing Letter:* Try the missing letter in every position, starting at the front and working your way through the word.

- *Transformers:* Look at the last word. Which letter from this word could be inserted in the first word to make a new word? Repeat until you get to the bottom.

Puzzle Hints *(cont.)*

Number Puzzles

- *Addition Tree:* If it doesn't work from the top down, try filling in the boxes from the bottom up.

- *Fill in the Blanks:* Start on the right, with the singles digit, and then work left.

- *In Addition:* If there are three numbers in any row or column, you can find the fourth number. Do those first.

- *It's Touching:* First, look for rows or columns that are missing only one number. Then, look for shaded numbers with only one blank box touching.

- *Math Path:* You will almost always add the greatest numbers. In longer puzzles, look for a path between the two greatest numbers that includes an addition sign for both.

- *Snake Race:* Keep in mind the numbers that add up to your target number. Then, look for one of those numbers in the puzzle. Start at that number and experiment with ways to move until you find the combination you need.

- *Sudoku:* If a row, column, or 2 x 2 box already contains three numbers, you can fill in the fourth. Fill those in before proceeding.

- *Thinking of a Number:* Work from the filled-in digit, if there is one.

Logic Puzzles

- *How Old?:* There are two things that have to be true. Try to figure out the first true thing, and then experiment with numbers that would also make the second thing true.

- *Kara's Kitten, Alice's Book, etc.:* Memorize the three things you are looking for (e.g., + collar, + short tail, + black feet). Then scan the puzzle in order, looking for the picture that matches the description.

- *Letter Box:* Use pencil to write all of the possibilities in each box, and then erase possibilities as you read the clues.

- *Mike, Anne, Fred, and Kate:* If three people did not do something, the fourth must have. If someone did something, it means that no one else did it and that he or she did not do anything else. (This will help you draw more **X**s on the chart.)

- *Odd Animal Out:* Think about starting letters, or look for things that three of the animals have in common. Maybe there's more than one answer!

- *What's Next?:* Look for the repeating pattern.

Shape Find

1

How many squares can you find in this picture? _____

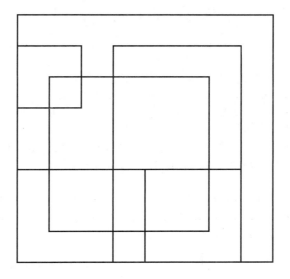

Fit It!

2

Fit all of the shapes into the square below. Either draw your answer, or trace and cut out the shapes before laying them on the square.

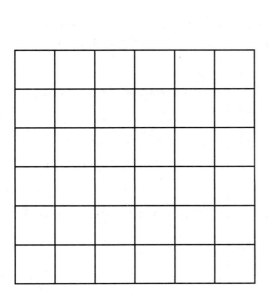

Solid Gold Game

3

Directions:

1. Find a partner, and cut out the first shape below.

2. Decide who goes first.

3. Take turns. You each get 30 seconds to try to fold the shape into a solid.

4. Whoever makes the solid first wins! Tape your solid together. If you have time, play again using the second shape!

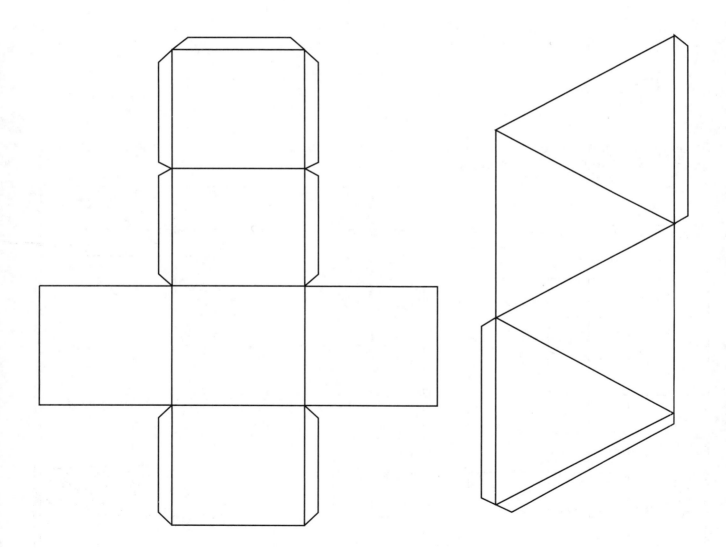

Shape Construction

4

Combine the shapes below to make a triangle.

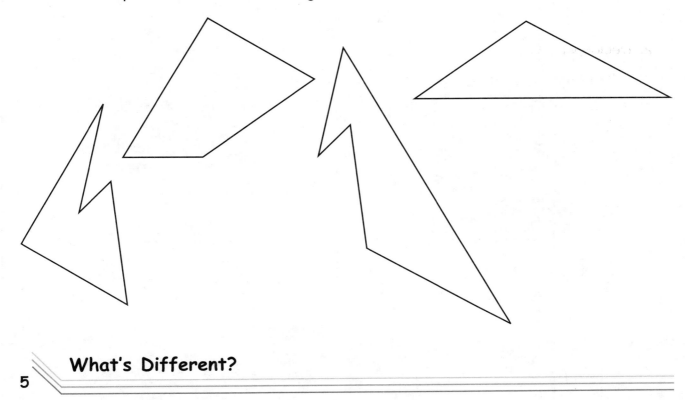

What's Different?

5

Can you spot the seven differences between these two pictures? Circle them.

Ad Match

6

Look at these old advertisements, and fill in the chart below.

Clue	Ad Number	What Is It?
It only costs twenty-five cents.		
You would use this to fix a broken toy.		
Cinnamon is one of them.		
You take this for a sore throat.		

Triangle Take-Away Game

7

Directions:

1. Find a partner.

2. Put a blank piece of paper over the picture below, and trace it lightly in pencil.

3. Take turns erasing a line. You can erase a full line or only a section that connects any other two lines. But, you must leave at least one triangle.

4. The first person who cannot leave one triangle on the board loses.

5. If you have time, trace the shape again and play another round!

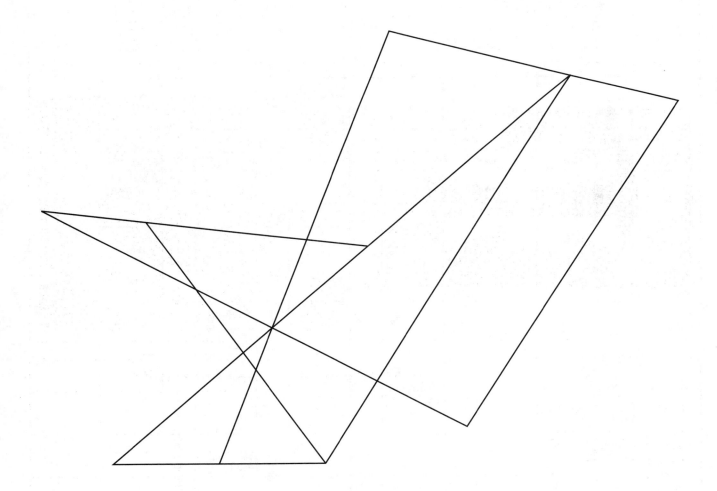

Map Madness!

8

Do you see Peter? He is lost! Follow the directions to get him back on track. Mark his ending spot with an **X**.

Directions:

1. ← Go west on Third Ave.
2. ← Go left on Peach St.
3. ← Go left on First Ave.
4. ← Go left on Plum St.
5. → Go right on Fifth Ave.

6. → Go right on Pear St.
7. ← Go left on Second Ave.
8. ← Go left on Orange St.
9. ← Go left on Third Ave.
10. **END** End at the corner of Peach St.

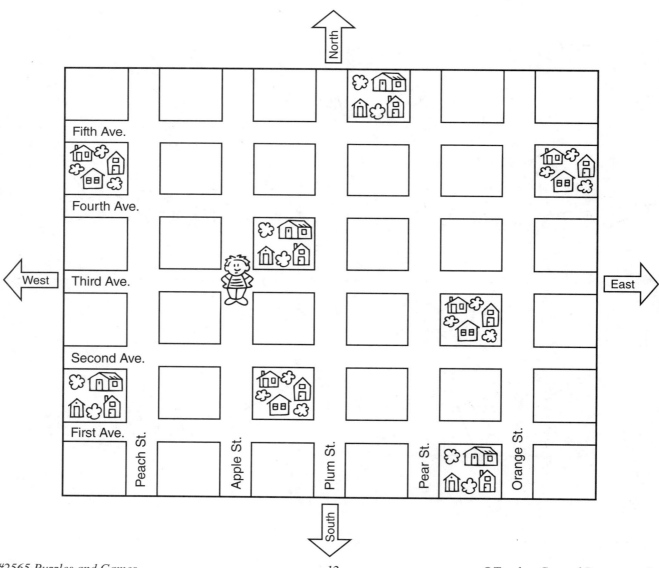

9 ⧅ Split Shapes

Can you draw one line on this shape to make four triangles? (*Note:* There will be other shapes remaining, and the line will cross sides.)

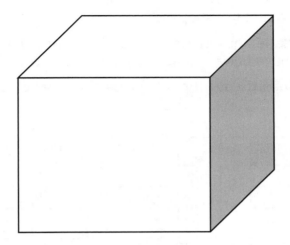

10 ⧅ Rebus

These are pictures of common sayings. What are the sayings?

BEill**D**	x**QQQ**me
little little **late late**	you*JUST*me

Shape Slap

11

Directions:

1. Find a partner.

2. Look at the game board and the shapes.

3. Take turns picking a shape and coloring it in on the board. If you need to, you can spin the shape. Once you have used a shape, put an **X** over its box.

4. The first person who doesn't have room to place a shape loses!

Shapes:

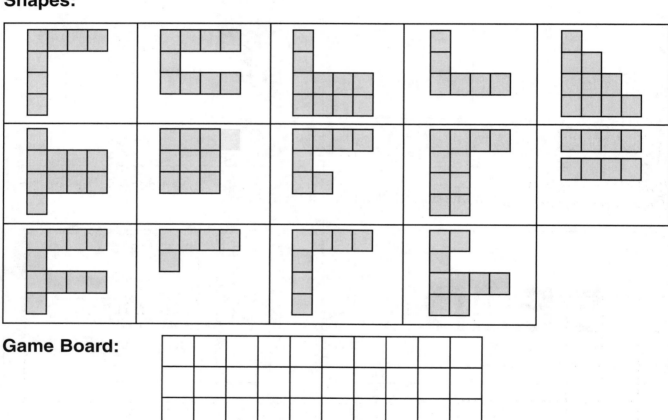

Game Board:

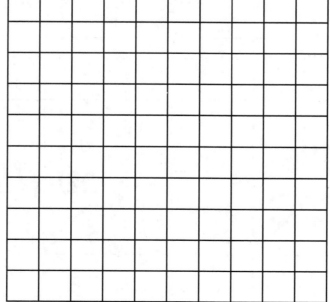

Split Shapes

12

Can you draw a rectangle on these shapes to make eight new triangles?

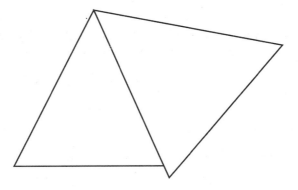

Fit It!

13

Fit all of the shapes into the square below. Either draw your answer, or trace and cut out the shapes before laying them on the square.

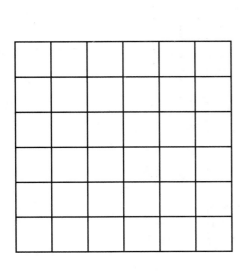

Shape Construction

14

Combine the shapes below to make a square.

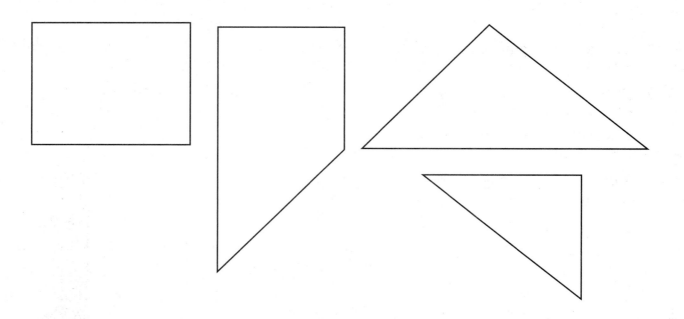

What's Different?

15

Can you spot the five differences between these two pictures? Circle them.

Tangram Game

Directions:

1. Find a partner. Each of you will need a copy of this sheet with your own set of shapes. Cut out the shapes in the square below.

2. Look at the tangram pictures below. When you say "go," you and your partner will race to make these pictures using all of your shapes.

3. Once one of you has made a picture, cross it out. This picture is now used. Both you and your partner should move on to the next picture.

4. Whoever makes the most pictures wins!

Shapes:

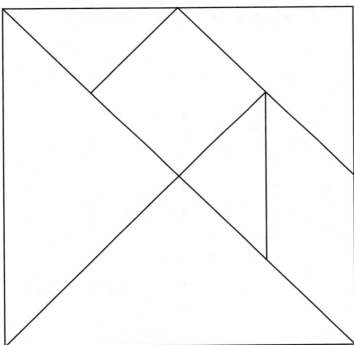

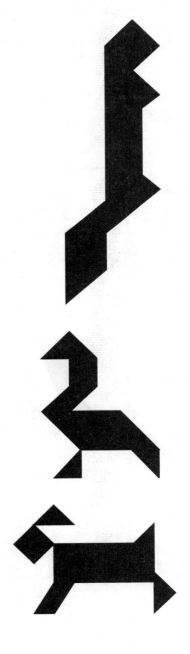

Tangram Pictures:

Map Madness!

Do you see Peter? He is lost again! Follow the directions to get him back on track. Mark his ending spot with an **X**.

Directions:

1. Go south on Whole St.

2. Go right on Adams Rd.

3. Go left on Quarter St.

4. Go right on Best Rd.

5. Go right on Half St.

6. Take Henry Rd. toward One-Fifth St.

7. Turn left on One-Third St.

8. Go two blocks and then take a right.

9. Take another right on Whole St.

10. **END** End at the corner of Best Rd.

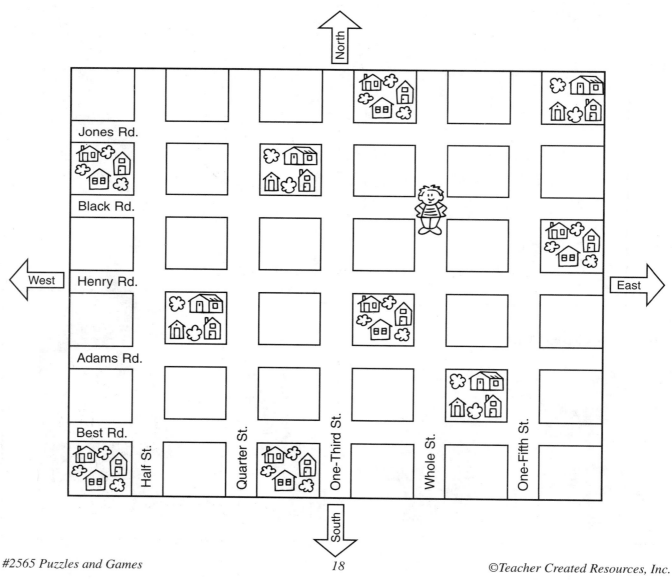

18 Rebus

These are pictures of common sayings. What are the sayings?

FUNNY FUNNY
WORDS WORDS
WORDS WORDS

BAN/ANA

_____

_____

19 Shape Find

How many circles can you find in this picture? _____

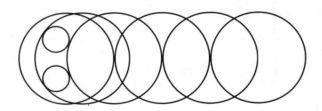

20 What's Different?

Can you spot the five differences between these two pictures? Circle them.

Cartoon Helpers

21

Directions:

1. Find a partner. You will each need a pencil.

2. Look at the boxes below. The first box shows the start of a cartoon.

3. Draw the next box. Then, have your partner write the caption for what you drew. Don't talk!

4. Now you will trade jobs: Your partner will draw the next box, and you will write the caption.

5. Take turns until all of the boxes are filled in.

6. At the end, work together to tell the complete story.

Pictures			
	ZOO		
Captions	Kim and Michael went to the zoo.		

Pictures			
Captions			

Split Shapes

22

Can you draw two lines to split this shape into five triangles and one rectangle?

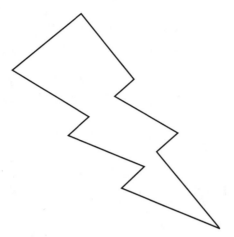

Fit It!

23

Fit all of the shapes into the square below. Either draw your answer, or trace and cut out the shapes before laying them on the square.

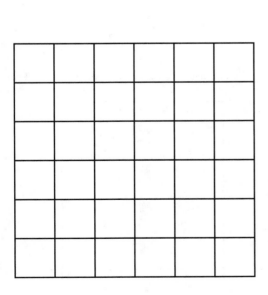

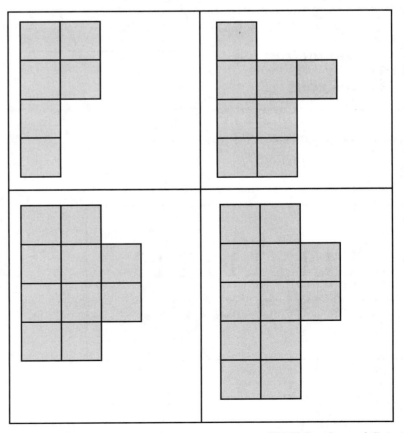

Shape Construction

24

Combine the shapes below to make a triangle.

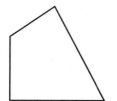 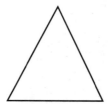 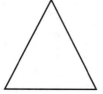 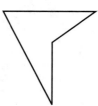

Shape Find

25

How many triangles can you find in this picture? _____

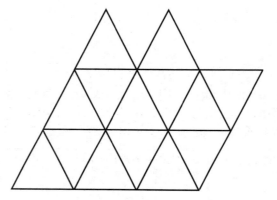

Rebus

26

These are pictures of common sayings.
What are the sayings?

1 1 1 1 1 1 1 1 1
4:45 a.m.

S
E
T
T
L
E

_____

Split Shapes

27

Can you draw a square that makes twenty-eight new triangles? (*Hint:* Don't draw inside the innermost square.)

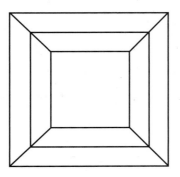

Solid Gold Game

28

Directions:

1. Find a partner, and cut out the first shape below.

2. Decide who goes first.

3. Take turns. You each get 30 seconds to try to fold the shape into a solid.

4. Whoever makes the solid first wins! Tape your solid together. If you have time, play again using the second shape!

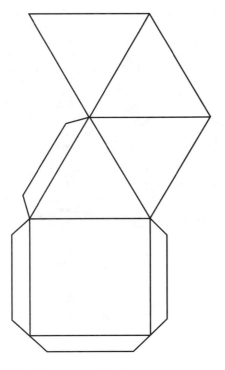

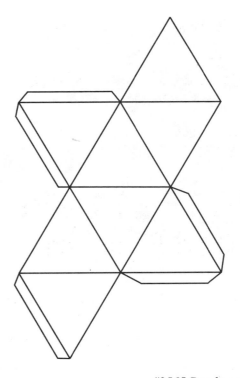

29 Rebus

These are pictures of common sayings. What are the sayings?

talk

stand

_____   _____

30 What's Different?

Can you spot the five differences between these two pictures? Circle them.

Shape Slap

Directions:

1. Find a partner.
2. Look at the game board and the shapes.
3. Take turns picking a shape and coloring it in on the game board. If you need to, you can spin the shape. Once you have used a shape, put an **X** over its box.
4. The first person who doesn't have room to place a shape loses!

Shapes:

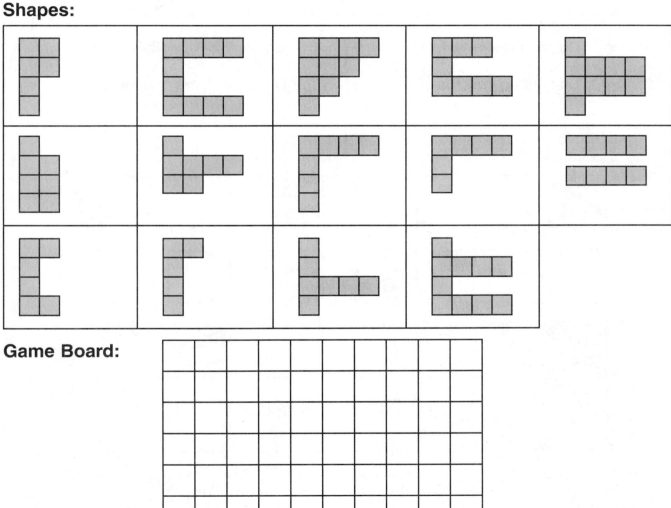

Game Board:

Do you see Peter? He is lost again! Follow the directions to get him back on track. Mark his ending spot with an **X**.

Directions:

1. Go east on Purple St.

2. Go right on Reed Ave.

3. Go left on Persimmon St.

4. Go left on Rode Ave.

5. Go right on Puce St.

6. Go left on Road Ave.

7. Go one block and take a left.

8. Go three blocks and take a right.

9. Go one block and take a right.

10. **END** Go three blocks and then stop.

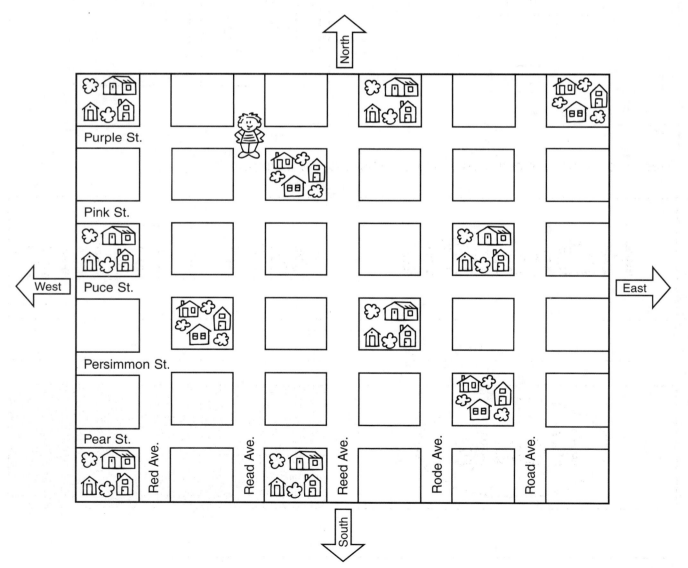

33 Fit It!

Fit all of the shapes into the square below. Either draw your answer, or trace and cut out the shapes before laying them on the square.

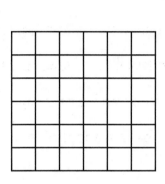

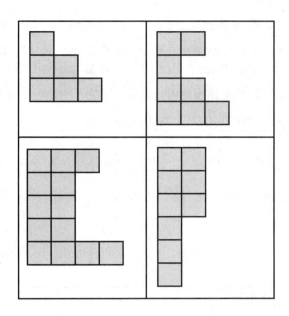

34 Rebus

These are pictures of common sayings. What are the sayings?

Triangle Take-Away Game

35

Directions:

1. Find a partner.

2. Put a blank piece of paper over the picture below, and trace it lightly in pencil.

3. Take turns erasing a line. You can erase a full line or only a section that connects any two other lines. But, you must leave at least one triangle.

4. The first person who cannot leave one triangle on the board loses.

5. If you have time, trace the shape again and play another round!

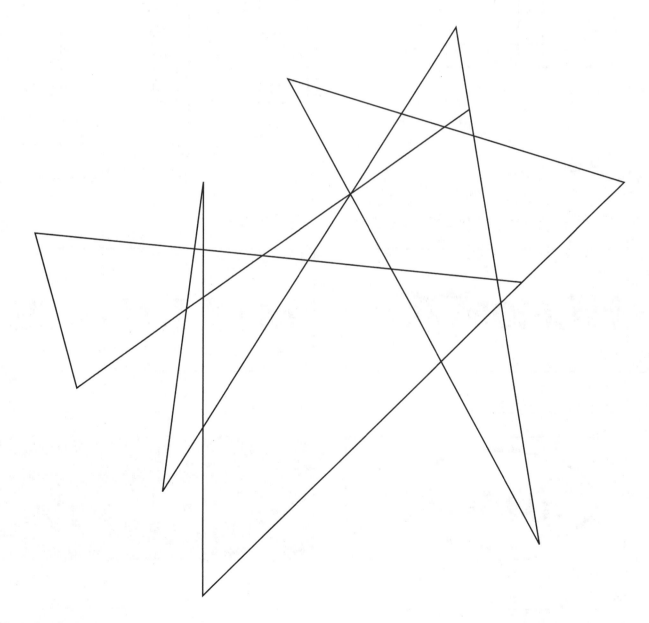

36 Transformers

Change one letter at a time to get from the top word to the bottom word. Each row must make a real word.

Example:

p	e	s	t
p	**o**	s	t
p	o	**e**	t
p	o	e	**m**

s	a	y	s
d	u	d	s

37 Missing Letter

The letter "l" has been taken out of the front, middle, or end of these words. The letter might be used more than once. What are the words?

amost: _____   itte: _____   ow: _____ ,

oipop: _____   spi: _____   _____

oi: _____   imitess: _____

38 Crossword

Read the clues and fill in the letters.

Across

1. A ship has a first _____ .
5. A sports figure might be one.
6. to mail a letter
7. poems, sometimes

Down

1. a type of soup
2. I _____ that test!
3. the sound of an instrument
4. the opposite of *begins*

1	2	3	4
5			
6			
7			

39 Hide and Seek

Can you find the three animals hiding in this sentence? Circle them.

Example: Help igloos!

Wait until the pan darkens to add sauce or risk unknown results.

40 Crack the Code

What kind of can never needs a can opener? Crack the code to find out!

a=1, b=2, c=3, d=4, e=5, f=6, etc.

1		16	5	12	9	3	1	14

41 Letter Scramble

Make words using all of these letters: mtae.

1. _____   3. _____

2. _____   4. _____

42 Before and After

Put a word in the blank boxes so that it makes a word or short phrase with the word in front and the word after.

Example:

S	P	E	L	L	I	N	G				H	I	V	E	= SPELLING BEE HIVE

	I	N				L	A	D	D	E	R

Rhyme Game

43

Directions:

1. Find a partner. Each player should use a different-colored pen. Then, look at the words below.

2. Race your partner to write rhymes for these words. Remember, words don't have to be spelled the same in order to rhyme!

3. Once you write a rhyme in a box, the box is closed.

4. Whoever closes the most boxes wins!

5. If you have time, work together to write a poem using some of these words.

blonde	still	pester
_____ rhyme	_____ rhyme	_____ rhyme
move	chain	hold
_____ rhyme	_____ rhyme	_____ rhyme
sunny	leaves	lunch
_____ rhyme	_____ rhyme	_____ rhyme
bread	lightning	snow
_____ rhyme	_____ rhyme	_____ rhyme

44 Hide and Seek

Can you find the same animal three times in this sentence? Circle it each time.

Example: Help igloos!

The sumo thundered in, trying to smother his mother's opponent.

45 Crack the Code

The student got in trouble for something he didn't do. What was it? Crack the code to find out!

z=1, a=2, b=3, c=4, d=5, etc.

9	10	20		9	16	14	6	24	16	19	12

46 Transformers

Change one letter at a time to get from the top word to the bottom word. Each row must make a real word.

Example:

p	e	s	t
p	**o**	s	t
p	o	**e**	t
p	o	e	**m**

p	i	g	s
t	o	e	s

47 Letter Scramble

Make three words using all of these letters: scldo.

1. _____

2. _____

3. _____

48 Transformers

Change one letter at a time to get from the top word to the bottom word. Each row must make a real word.

Example:

p	e	s	t
p	**o**	s	t
p	o	**e**	t
p	o	e	**m**

m	i	s	t
l	a	s	h

49 Missing Letter

The letter "p" has been taken out of the front, middle, or end of these words. The letter might be used more than once. What are the words?

aer: _____   retty: _____

roer: _____   roose: _____

aear: _____   um:_____ , _____

Crossword Challenge

50

Directions:

1. Using different-colored pens, work with a partner to put these words into the crossword puzzle. Each word must touch at least one other word.

2. Now, take turns adding new words to the puzzle. Be creative!

3. The person who can add the most new words wins.

4. Once you have finished the game, write clues for your answers. Make a crossword board with numbers that match your answers. Ask a friend to solve your crossword puzzle!

| anteater | fauna | manta |
| orangutan | macaw | tiger |

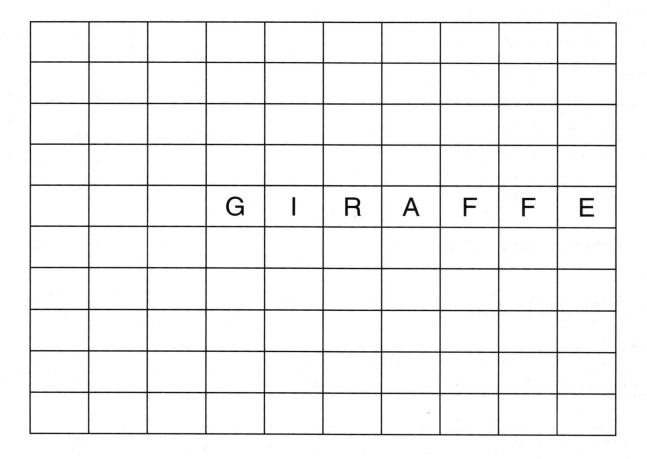

51 Letter Scramble

Make three words using all of these letters: Ista.

1. _____

2. _____

3. _____

52 Crossword

Read the clues and fill in the letters.

Across

1. a picky person
5. A pimple can be caused by a clogged
_____.
6. He wants a hole, so he _____ a shovel.
7. the opposite of *hard work*

Down

1. It is on the back of a cowboy's boot.
2. You have one in the middle of your face.
3. metals, before they are refined
4. the opposite of *worst*

1	2	3	4
5			
6			
7			

53 Before and After

Put a word in the blank boxes so that it makes a word or short phrase with the word in front and the word after.

Example:

| S | P | E | L | L | I | N | G | | | H | I | V | E |

= SPELLING BEE HIVE

| S | C | A | P | E | | | | H | E | R | D |

Crack the Code

54

What kind of monkey can fly? Crack the code to find out!

a=3, b=4, c=5, d=6, etc.

3	■	10	17	22	■	3	11	20	■	4	3	4	17	17	16

Hide and Seek

55

Can you find the three animals hiding in this sentence? Circle them.

Example: Help igloos!

My amigo ate microwaved chili on toast.

Letter Scramble

56

Make two words using all of these letters: trhae.

1. _____   2. _____

Before and After

57

Put a word in the blank boxes so that it makes a word or short phrase with the word in front and the word after.

Example:

S	P	E	L	L	I	N	G			H	I	V	E

= SPELLING BEE HIVE

G	R	E	E	N					N	A	I	L

Beginnings and Ends Game

Directions:

1. Find a partner.

2. Look at the pictures below. Think of the words they show.

3. Start at *mitten*. This word ends with the letter "n." Which word begins with the letter "n"? The first one has been done for you.

4. Take turns drawing arrows to the next picture. Also, write the words you use.

5. If you cannot find a word in one minute, your partner wins. If you use every picture, you both win!

Hide and Seek

59

Can you find the two animals hiding in this sentence? Circle them.

Example: Help igloos!

Come watch Harmonica Mel fulfill amateur dreams.

Crossword

60

Read the clues and fill in the letters.

Across

1. It carries blood.

5. a measure of land (like a square mile)

6. The circus performer _____ out of the cannon.

7. An elephant can weigh five _____ .

Down

1. huge—rhymes with *last*

2. your voice, bouncing back

3. You do it to clothes.

4. They hang from basketball hoops.

1	2	3	4
5			
6			
7			

Missing Letter

61

The letter "e" has been taken out of the front, middle, or end of these words. The letter might be used more than once. What are the words?

jct: _____

lft: _____

nrgtic: _____

l: _____ , _____

w: _____ , _____

flt: _____ , _____

Before and After

62

Put a word in the blank boxes so that it makes a word or short phrase with the word in front and the word after.

Example:

| S | P | E | L | L | I | N | G | | | | H | I | V | E | = SPELLING BEE HIVE |

| H | O | T | | | | P | O | R | T |

Letter Scramble

63

Make two words using all of these letters: hsuto.

1. _____   2. _____

Hide and Seek

64

Can you find the six animals hiding in this sentence? Circle them.

Example: Help igloos!

The trapeze brat scowled while arresting Ray.

Crack the Code

65

What does a sea monster like to eat? Crack the code to find out!

a=26, b=25, c=24, d=23, e=22, etc.

| | | | | ■ | | | | ■ | | | | | |
| 21 | 18 | 8 | 19 | | 26 | 13 | 23 | | 8 | 19 | 18 | 11 | 8 |

Changing Letters
66

Directions:

1. Find a partner. Start with the word below.

2. Change one letter to make a new word. Write this word in the next row.

3. Take turns. You cannot use a word more than once.

4. If you cannot make a new word, you are out. If you reach the end of the puzzle together, you both win!

Example:

p	a	n
p	**i**	n
p	i	**g**
b	i	g

Start	h	o	s	e
1.				
2.				
3.				
4.				
5.				
6.				
7.				
8.				
9.				
10.				

Hide and Seek

67

Can you find the three animals hiding in this sentence?   Circle them.

Example: Help igloos!

"Isn't baseball amazing?" asked Catherine, her cornea gleaming.

Missing Letter

68

The letter "b" has been taken out of the front, middle, or end of these words. The letter might be used more than once. What are the words?

ule: _____

aseall: _____

areviation: _____

hoy: _____

huu: _____

asor: _____

end: _____

Transformers

69

Change one letter at a time to get from the top word to the bottom word. Each row must make a real word.

Example:

p	e	s	t
p	**o**	s	t
p	o	**e**	t
p	o	e	**m**

s	t	o	p
c	h	o	w

70 Crossword

Read the clues and fill in the letters.

Across

1. went in circles
5. ice-cream _____
6. A sparrow is ____ ____ ____ ____ tle bird.
7. If fruit sits in the sun too long, it _____ .

Down

1. A deep cut could leave a _____.
2. a game played on horses
3. The class started a new _____ about planets.
4. They hang from basketball hoops.

1	2	3	4
5			
6			
7			

71 Letter Scramble

Make three words using all of these letters: rtsea.

1. _____

2. _____

3. _____

72 Before and After

Put a word in the blank boxes so that it makes a word or short phrase with the word in front and the word after.

Example:

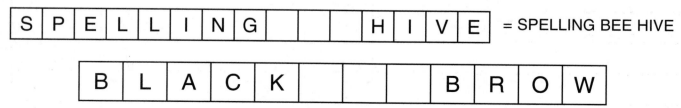

| S | P | E | L | L | I | N | G | | | H | I | V | E | = SPELLING BEE HIVE |

| B | L | A | C | K | | | B | R | O | W |

Fronts and Backs

73

Directions:

1. These letters are the "fronts" and "backs" of words.
2. Find a partner.
3. Take turns writing words. Make a word using the "fronts" and "backs" provided. Write it in your space.
4. If you cannot make a new word, you are out.
5. The person with the most words wins!

Fronts	Backs
re	sting
assi	ise
coa	gn
ru	sts
tru	ch
li	ts
disgu	uther
cru	ck
boa	mpet
prom	th

Player #1	Player #2

Crack the Code

74

What city has no people? Crack the code to find out!

a=1, b=3, c=2, d=4, e=5, f=7, g=6, h=8, i=9, etc.

5	12	5	2	20	19	9	2	9	20	25

Hide and Seek

75

Can you find the four animals hiding in this sentence? Circle them.

Example: Help igloos!

The crowds abhor selfish AM stereo use.

Transformers

76

Change one letter at a time to get from the top word to the bottom word. Each row must make a real word.

Example:

p	e	s	t
p	**o**	s	t
p	o	**e**	t
p	o	e	**m**

s	p	i	n
p	l	o	t

Before and After

77

Put a word in the blank boxes so that it makes a word or short phrase with the word in front and the word after.

Example:

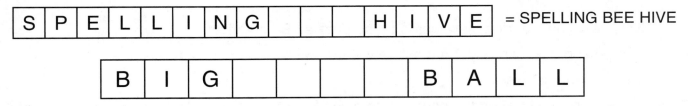

| S | P | E | L | L | I | N | G | | | H | I | V | E | = SPELLING BEE HIVE |

| B | I | G | | | | B | A | L | L |

Crossword

78

Read the clues and fill in the letters.

Across

1. The snow _____ cleared the road.
5. The actress forgot her _____.
6. You cook in it.
7. The scientist used a _____ tube.

Down

1. a story line
2. Where do you _____?
3. They come before *twos*.
4. She _____ to the store.

1	2	3	4
5			
6			
7			

Missing Letter

79

The letter "d" has been taken out of the front, middle, or end of these words. The letter might be used more than once. What are the words?

a: _____ , _____   ae: _____

o: _____ , _____   granay: _____

i: _____   weing: _____

u: _____

Crossword Challenge

80

Directions:

1. Using different-colored pens, work with a partner to put these words into the crossword puzzle. Each word must touch at least one other word. If your letters make two new words, that's okay.

2. Now, take turns adding new words to the puzzle. Be creative!

3. The person who can add the most new words wins.

4. Which planet is missing? _____

5. Once you have finished the game, write clues for your answers. Make a crossword board with numbers that match your answers. Ask a friend to solve your crossword puzzle!

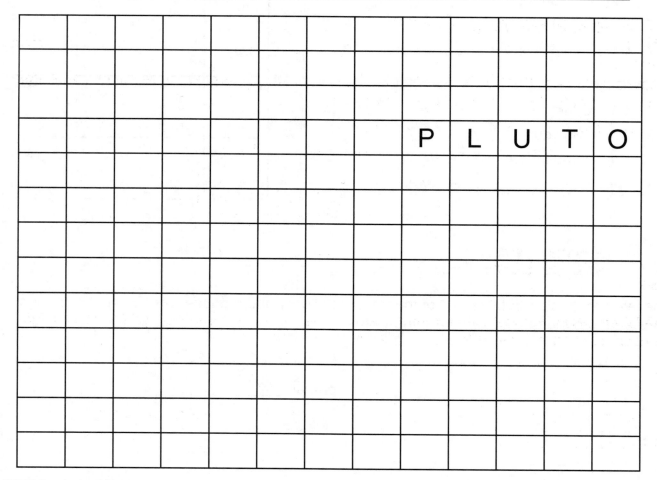

81 Hide and Seek

Can you find the three animals hiding in this sentence? Circle them.

Example: Help igloos!

Is the yeti German, or is Catherine gullible?

82 Letter Scramble

Make three words using all of these letters: crea.

1. _____

2. _____

3. _____

83 Crack the Code

What seven letters did Old Mother Hubbard say when she opened her cupboard? Crack the code to find out!   (*Hint:* The answer is a code, too!)

a=1, e=2, i=3, o=4, u=5, b=6, c=7, d=8, f=9, etc.

4	3	7	5	19	15	21

84 Missing Letter

The letter "f" has been taken out of the front, middle, or end of these words. The letter might be used more than once. What are the words?

lu: _____ , _____   aect: _____

ater: _____   act: _____

eort: _____

Transformers

85

Change one letter at a time to get from the top word to the bottom word. Each row must make a real word.

Example:

p	e	s	t
p	**o**	s	t
p	o	**e**	t
p	o	e	**m**

s	c	o	l	d
s	h	a	r	e

Letter Scramble

86

Make two words using all of these letters: rtswa.

1. _____   2. _____

Crossword

87

Read the clues and fill in the letters.

Across

1. Welcome to the _____!
5. The left one on the freeway is fast.
6. a liquid that burns
7. Dogs, cats, and hamsters are _____.

Down

1. to bring your hands together
2. a shoe string
3. The class started a new _____ about grammar.
4. Some people sleep in bunk _____ .

1	2	3	4
5			
6			
7			

Changing Letters

88

Directions:

1. Find a partner. Start with the word below.

2. Change one letter to make a new word. Write the word in the next row.

3. Take turns. You cannot use a word more than once.

4. If you cannot make a new word, you are out. If you reach the end of the puzzle together, you both win!

Example:

p	a	n
p	**i**	n
p	i	**g**
b	i	g

Start	h	a	n	d
1.				
2.				
3.				
4.				
5.				
6.				
7.				
8.				
9.				
10.				

89 Letter Scramble

Make four words using all of these letters: plas.

1. _____   3. _____

2. _____   4. _____

90 Missing Letter

The letter "g" has been taken out of the front, middle, or end of these words. The letter might be used more than once. What are the words?

jule: _____   ilin: _____

rude: _____   zizain: _____

ae: _____   oles: _____

e: _____

91 Hide and Seek

Can you find the five animals hiding in this sentence? Circle them.

Example: Help igloos!

The overcrowded wheelbarrow led to a difficult size brawl.

92 Before and After

Put a word in the blank boxes so that it makes a word or short phrase with the word in front and the word after.

Example:

| S | P | E | L | L | I | N | G | | | H | I | V | E | = SPELLING BEE HIVE |

| | B | A | D | | | | H | E | A | D | |

93 Transformers

Change one letter at a time to get from the top word to the bottom word. Each row must make a real word.

Example:

p	e	s	t
p	**o**	s	t
p	o	**e**	t
p	o	e	**m**

g	i	r	l	s
p	o	l	e	s

94 Letter Scramble

Make three words using all of these letters: staco.

1. _____

2. _____

3. _____

95 Crossword

Read the clues and fill in the letters.

Across

1. the opposite of *hard*
5. the elbow-like joint in your leg
6. When a boy burns his hand, he _____ it.
7. If it is hot, the answer for clue #6 will _____ .

Down

1. milk with the least fat
2. _____ upon a time
3. If you _____ sick, stay home.
4. If you study, you will do well on the _____ .

1	2	3	4
5			
6			
7			

96 Letter Scramble

Make four words using all of these letters: lstea.

1. _____   3. _____

2. _____   4. _____

97 Hide and Seek

Can you find the three animals hiding in this sentence? Circle them.

Example: Help igloos!

"The slob's terrified to hang up pylons!" said his mother.

98 Letter Scramble

Make three words using all of these letters: fteas.

1. _____

2. _____

3. _____

99 Before and After

Put a word in the blank boxes so that it makes a word or short phrase with the word in front and the word after.

Example:

| S | P | E | L | L | I | N | G | | | H | I | V | E | = SPELLING BEE HIVE |

| F | O | R | E | | | C | H | A | I | R |

100 Sudoku

Each row, column, and 2 x 2 box has the digits 1, 2, 3, and 4. Fill in the blanks to complete the puzzle.

4	2	1	3
1		4	
	4		1
2	1	3	

101 In Addition

Fill in the blanks with the digits 1–9 so that the sum of each row is the number to the right and the sum of each column is the number below it.

	7	8	6	25
4				14
		5	2	12
2		9	8	22
13	17	24	19	

Addition Tree
102

Put numbers in the boxes so that all of the boxes add up to the number they came from.

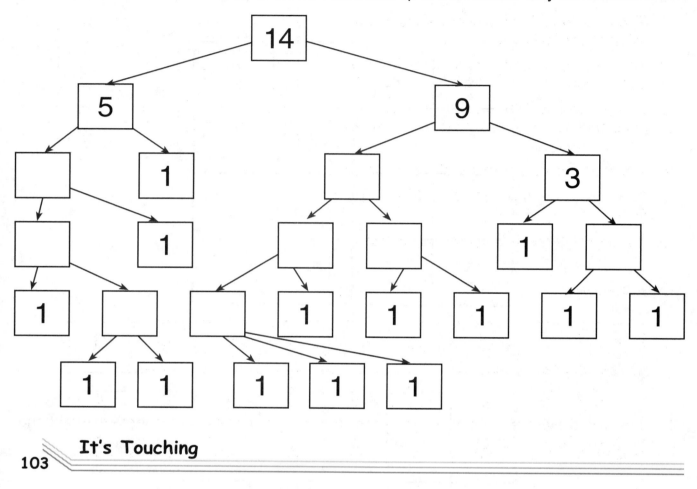

It's Touching
103

Fill in the blank boxes with the numbers 1–5. Each full row and column contains the numbers 1, 2, 3, 4, and 5. Each shaded number is the sum of all the numbers touching it.

4	1	5		
	26		23	3
3		4	2	1
5	25	2	23	4
2	3	1	4	

Snake Race

104

Directions:

1. Find a partner. Each player should use a different-colored pen.

2. Sit side by side, and put the game board in front of you.

3. Look for snakes that equal twenty-four. The numbers have to be touching. (You cannot jump around.)

4. You may use a number more than once.

5. Take turns. You have 30 seconds to find a snake.

6. If you cannot find a snake in 30 seconds, the other person wins.

Example:

5	+	7	+
+	8	+	12
7	+	6	+
+	9	+	9

Game Board:

48	÷	2	+	14	+	8	x	3
–	3	+	20	+	1	+	3	x
24	÷	8	x	8	x	3	x	6
–	14	–	8	x	12	–	2	+
18	+	1	+	1	+	4	x	6
x	6	+	9	+	14	+	9	+
4	+	17	+	8	–	4	+	8
–	2	x	12	+	2	+	6	+
2	+	2	–	10	x	4	x	4

Math Path

105

Pick the best starting number, and then go up/down or left/right until you have touched all of the numbers once. What is the *highest* total you can calculate? Draw your path.

6	+	5
+	3	−
2	−	4

Total: _____

Sudoku

106

Each row, column, and 2 x 2 box has the digits 1, 2, 3, and 4. Fill in the blanks to complete the puzzle.

4		1	2
1	2	4	
	4	3	1
3	1		4

107 Fill in the Blanks

Fill in the blanks to make this equation true.

$$
\begin{array}{r}
\square\,4\,\square \\
+\ 4\ 7\ 3 \\
\hline
6\ \square\ 7
\end{array}
$$

108 Thinking of a Number

I'm thinking of a four-digit number in which:
- the sum of the first and second digits is nine.
- the sum of the third and fourth digits is nine.
- the sum of the second and third digits is eleven.
- the fourth digit is smaller than the first.

109 In Addition

Fill in the blanks with the digits 1–9 so that the sum of each row is the number to the right, and the sum of each column is the number below it.

2	9		7	23
3	6			14
			9	20
5	9		2	23
16	27	15	22	

Tic-Tac-Toe Race

110

Directions:

1. Pick a colored pen. Have your partner pick a different color.
2. Choose a tic-tac-toe board, and sit side by side.
3. Start at the same time, and race to solve the math problems. (You might want to use scrap paper.)
4. When you solve a problem, write the answer in the box.
5. If you get three in a row, you win.
6. Check your answers. If your partner wrote a wrong answer, the space is yours!

Example:

6 − 4	4 + 2	8 − 3
9 + 5 14	4 + 5	2 + 7
1 + 6	3 + 9	7 − 5

Game Boards:

325 − 172	228 + 449	21 x 8
14 x 19	240 ÷ 15	164 − 87
150 ÷ 3	472 + 598	243 ÷ 9

153 ÷ 17	812 + 94	19 x 8
634 + 436	322 ÷ 23	24 x 28
32 x 35	756 − 348	13 x 13

6 x 16	4 x 14	9 x 19
2 x 12	598 ÷ 26	8 x 18
7 x 17	3 x 13	5 x 15

342 ÷ 38	674 + 249	783 ÷ 29
72 − 34	34 + 17	4 x 9
27 x 31	15 x 18	18 x 26

Sudoku

Each row, column, and 2 x 2 box has the digits 1, 2, 3, and 4. Fill in the blanks to complete the puzzle.

2	4		
4		3	1
3	1		2

In Addition

Fill in the blanks with the digits 1–9 so that the sum of each row is the number to the right, and the sum of each column is the number below it.

	6		4	22
	7	2	8	19
	9	3		23
6			9	25
19	29	16	25	

113 Fill in the Blanks

Fill in the blanks to make this equation true.

$$
\begin{array}{ccc}
  & 2 & \square & \square \\
+ & \square & 4 & 9 \\
\hline
  & 5 & 2 & 8 \\
\end{array}
$$

114 Math Path

Pick the best starting number, and then go up/down or left/right until you have touched all of the numbers once. What is the *highest* total you can calculate? Draw your path.

5	+	1
–	2	–
1	+	2

Total: _____

115 It's Touching

Fill in the blank boxes with the numbers 1–5. Each full row and column contains the numbers 1, 2, 3, 4, and 5. Each shaded number is the sum of all the numbers touching it.

4	1			5
2	22	1	20	3
		2	3	
1	28		22	4
3		5	1	2

Meet Your Match

116

Directions:

1. Find a partner. Each of you will need a copy of this sheet and a different-colored pen.

2. Look at the left and right sides in the columns below. On each side, there are equations that have the same answer.

3. Draw lines between equations that have the same answer. The first one has been done for you.

4. The person who can make the most matches wins.

834 ÷ 417	268 ÷ 67
117 ÷ 39	504 ÷ 8
224 ÷ 56	259 ÷ 37
225 ÷ 45	243 + 987
6 x 24	18 ÷ 6
17 x 32	8 x 68
13 x 28	402 ÷ 67
14 x 44	22 x 28
9 x 72	3 x 95
15 x 43	348 ÷ 174
534 ÷ 89	8 x 18
19 x 15	5 x 129
9 x 7	984 – 979
4 + 3	6 x 108
358 + 872	14 x 26

117 Sudoku

Each row, column, and 2 x 2 box has the digits 1, 2, 3, and 4. Fill in the blanks to complete the puzzle.

	1	4	
4			2
1			4
	4	2	

118 Thinking of a Number

I'm thinking of a four-digit number in which:
- the sum of all four digits is twenty-six.
- the first and second digits are one apart.
- the second and third digits are one apart.
- from left to right, the digits get smaller.

119 Addition Tree

Put numbers in the boxes so that all of the boxes add up to the number they came from.

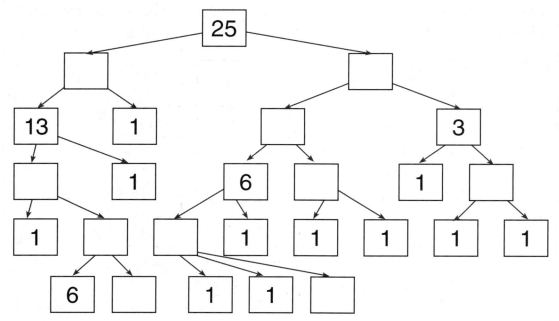

Fill in the Blanks
120

Fill in the blanks to make this equation true.

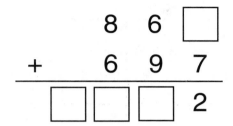

```
        8  6  □

   +    6  9  7
   _____
     □  □  □  2
```

Math Path
121

Pick the best starting number, and then go up/down or left/right until you have touched all of the numbers once. What is the *highest* total you can calculate? Draw your path.

16	+	5
−	9	−
8	−	12

Total: _____

In Addition
122

Fill in the blanks with the digits 1–9 so that the sum of each row is the number to the right, and the sum of each column is the number below it.

7	4		1	15
		9	6	21
2	6			15
	5	2		10
15	16	17	13	

Plus or Minus Game

123

Directions:

1. Find a partner. Each of you will need a copy of this sheet and a different-colored pen.

2. Look at the rows below. In each row, you have to add or subtract to get from the first number to the last. The first one has been done for you.

3. Race your partner to solve the rows. You do not have to go in order. The person who solves the most rows wins.

4. Ready, set, go!

| 16 | (+) or − | 3 | + or (−) | 9 | (+) or − | 5 | = | 15 |

| 67 | + or − | 22 | + or − | 9 | + or − | 34 | = | 20 |

| 82 | + or − | 13 | + or − | 67 | + or − | 19 | = | 47 |

| 18 | + or − | 76 | + or − | 47 | + or − | 19 | = | 28 |

| 44 | + or − | 36 | + or − | 7 | + or − | 98 | = | 99 |

| 57 | + or − | 17 | + or − | 23 | + or − | 76 | = | 93 |

| 40 | + or − | 13 | + or − | 12 | + or − | 14 | = | 53 |

| 76 | + or − | 57 | + or − | 9 | + or − | 87 | = | 97 |

124 Thinking of a Number

I'm thinking of a four-digit number in which:
- from left to right, the digits are in ascending order (one apart).
- the sum of all digits is eighteen.

125 It's Touching

Fill in the blank boxes with the numbers 1–5. Each full row and column contains the numbers 1, 2, 3, 4, and 5. Each shaded number is the sum of all the numbers touching it.

1		2		4
	17		25	3
	1	3	2	
5	26	4	26	1
3	1			2

126 Sudoku

Each row, column, and 3 x 2 box has the digits 1, 2, 3, 4, 5, and 6. Fill in the blanks to complete the puzzle.

		5			
	1	2	5	3	
	3	4	6	5	1
6	5	1	2	4	
	2	3	4	6	
			3		

In Addition

127

Fill in the blanks with the digits 1–9 so that the sum of each row is the number to the right, and the sum of each column is the number below it.

6			7	15
	3	1		12
	9	7		20
8			2	21

24	19	14	11

Addition Tree

128

Put numbers in the boxes so that all of the boxes add up to the number they came from.

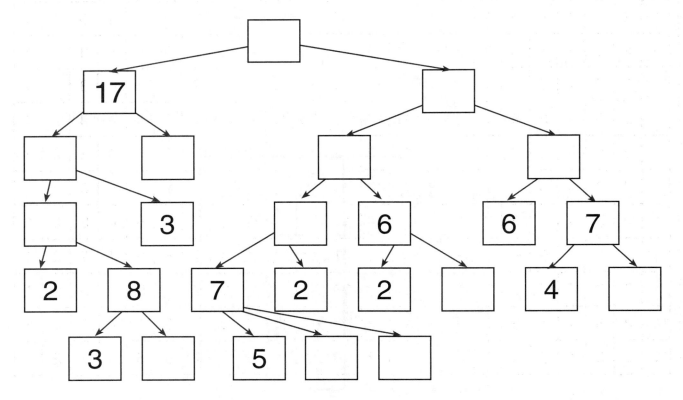

66

Addition Challenge
129

Directions:

1. Pick a colored pen. Have your partner pick a different color.

2. One player is on the left, and one player is on the right.

3. Look at the numbers in the middle. In each row, circle the numbers on your side that add up to the number in the middle. You can circle as many numbers as you need. For example:

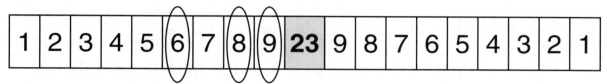

4. Once you have circled any combination of numbers, put an **X** on the number in the middle. That row is now closed. You get a point for each **X**.

5. Start at the same time, and solve as many rows as you can before your partner.

6. You do not have to solve the rows in order. (You can start at the end or skip around.)

7. At the end, the person with the most points wins.

Player #1												Player #2									
1	2	3	4	5	6	7	8	9	11	13	**52**	13	11	9	8	7	6	5	4	3	2	1
1	2	3	4	5	6	7	8	9	11	13	**45**	13	11	9	8	7	6	5	4	3	2	1
1	2	3	4	5	6	7	8	9	11	13	**49**	13	11	9	8	7	6	5	4	3	2	1
1	2	3	4	5	6	7	8	9	11	13	**32**	13	11	9	8	7	6	5	4	3	2	1
1	2	3	4	5	6	7	8	9	11	13	**63**	13	11	9	8	7	6	5	4	3	2	1
1	2	3	4	5	6	7	8	9	11	13	**56**	13	11	9	8	7	6	5	4	3	2	1
1	2	3	4	5	6	7	8	9	11	13	**19**	13	11	9	8	7	6	5	4	3	2	1
1	2	3	4	5	6	7	8	9	11	13	**47**	13	11	9	8	7	6	5	4	3	2	1
1	2	3	4	5	6	7	8	9	11	13	**58**	13	11	9	8	7	6	5	4	3	2	1
1	2	3	4	5	6	7	8	9	11	13	**60**	13	11	9	8	7	6	5	4	3	2	1
1	2	3	4	5	6	7	8	9	11	13	**40**	13	11	9	8	7	6	5	4	3	2	1

130 Fill in the Blanks

Fill in the blanks to make this equation true.

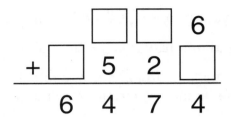

$$
\begin{array}{r}
\square\,\square\,6 \\
+\ \square\ 5\ 2\ \square \\
\hline
6\ 4\ 7\ 4
\end{array}
$$

131 Sudoku

Each row, column, and 3 x 2 box has the digits 1, 2, 3, 4, 5, and 6. Fill in the blanks to complete the puzzle.

	6	3		4	
4	5		1	6	3
	1				6
6				1	
5	2	1		3	4
	4		5	2	

132 In Addition

Fill in the blanks with the digits 1–9 so that the sum of each row is the number to the right, and the sum of each column is the number below it.

4		3		25
1	5		7	17
	2		3	12
3				15

10	20	14	25

133 It's Touching

Fill in the blank boxes with the numbers 1–5. Each full row and column contains the numbers 1, 2, 3, 4, and 5. Each shaded number is the sum of all the numbers touching it.

5		2	3	1
3	25	1	21	5
			3	
	25		27	3
			3	4

134 Thinking of a Number

I'm thinking of a four-digit number in which:

- the digits are all the same.
- the sum of the digits is thirty-two.

135 Math Path

Pick the best starting number, and then go up/down or left/right until you have touched all of the numbers once. What is the *highest* total you can calculate? Draw your path.

18	–	1
–	22	–
7	+	6

Total: _____

Snake Race

136

Directions:

1. Find a partner. Each player should use a different-colored pen.

2. Sit side by side, and put the game board in front of you.

3. Look for snakes that equal thirty-two. The numbers have to be touching. (You cannot jump around.)

4. You may use a number more than once.

5. Take turns. You have 30 seconds to find a snake.

6. If you cannot find a snake in 30 seconds, the other person wins.

Example:

15	+	7	+
+	8	+	10
12	+	11	+
+	12	+	9

Game Board:

16	+	8	+	8	–	5	x	4
x	34	–	2	+	27	+	3	+
3	–	8	+	2	+	2	x	12
–	8	–	34	+	4	+	5	–
16	+	12	+	28	–	4	–	6
+	4	x	30	–	20	x	13	+
18	–	2	÷	2	+	4	x	2
+	2	+	2	x	16	x	16	+
12	x	8	+	30	+	2	+	14

137 Sudoku

Each row, column, and 3 x 2 box has the digits 1, 2, 3, 4, 5, and 6. Fill in the blanks to complete the puzzle.

1			4		3
	4	3		2	
5		1	2	4	
	6	4	3		5
	1		6	5	
4		6			2

138 Addition Tree

Put numbers in the boxes so that all of the boxes add up to the number they came from.

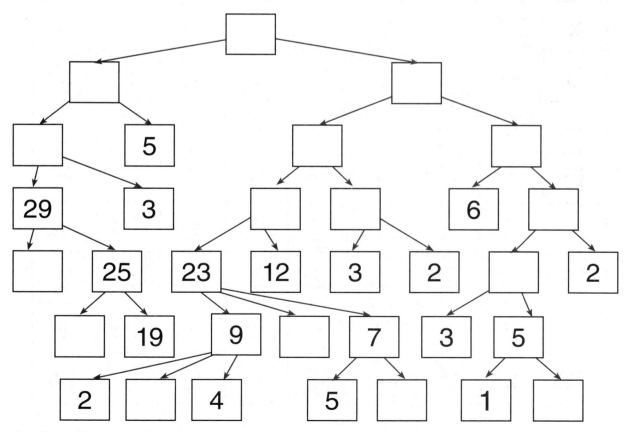

139 Fill in the Blanks

Fill in the blanks to make this equation true.

$$
\begin{array}{ccccc}
 & & \square & \square & 5 \\
+ & 3 & 7 & 6 & 6 \\
\hline
 & \square & 3 & 3 & \square \\
\end{array}
$$

140 Thinking of a Number

I'm thinking of a four-digit number in which:
- by multiplying digits together, there are two ways to get twenty-four.
- left to right, the digits get bigger.

141 In Addition

Fill in the blanks with the digits 1–9 so that the sum of each row is the number to the right, and the sum of each column is the number below it.

			4	16
3		6	2	16
2	8			28
	8			16
14	25	17	20	

Addition Challenge

142

Directions:

1. Pick a colored pen. Have your partner pick a different color.

2. One player is on the left, and one player is on the right.

3. Look at the numbers in the middle. In each row, circle numbers on your side that add up to the number in the middle. You can circle as many numbers as you need. For example:

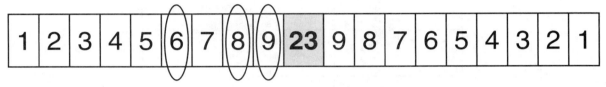

4. Once you have circled any combination of numbers, put an **X** on the number in the middle. That row is now closed. You get a point for each **X**.

5. Start at the same time, and solve as many rows as you can before your partner.

6. You do not have to solve the rows in order. (You can start at the end or skip around.)

7. At the end, the person with the most points wins.

Player #1														Player #2										
1	2	3	4	5	6	7	8	9	11	13	15	**56**	15	13	11	9	8	7	6	5	4	3	2	1
1	2	3	4	5	6	7	8	9	11	13	15	**63**	15	13	11	9	8	7	6	5	4	3	2	1
1	2	3	4	5	6	7	8	9	11	13	15	**38**	15	13	11	9	8	7	6	5	4	3	2	1
1	2	3	4	5	6	7	8	9	11	13	15	**44**	15	13	11	9	8	7	6	5	4	3	2	1
1	2	3	4	5	6	7	8	9	11	13	15	**71**	15	13	11	9	8	7	6	5	4	3	2	1
1	2	3	4	5	6	7	8	9	11	13	15	**47**	15	13	11	9	8	7	6	5	4	3	2	1
1	2	3	4	5	6	7	8	9	11	13	15	**53**	15	13	11	9	8	7	6	5	4	3	2	1
1	2	3	4	5	6	7	8	9	11	13	15	**19**	15	13	11	9	8	7	6	5	4	3	2	1
1	2	3	4	5	6	7	8	9	11	13	15	**36**	15	13	11	9	8	7	6	5	4	3	2	1
1	2	3	4	5	6	7	8	9	11	13	15	**50**	15	13	11	9	8	7	6	5	4	3	2	1
1	2	3	4	5	6	7	8	9	11	13	15	**69**	15	13	11	9	8	7	6	5	4	3	2	1
1	2	3	4	5	6	7	8	9	11	13	15	**62**	15	13	11	9	8	7	6	5	4	3	2	1
1	2	3	4	5	6	7	8	9	11	13	15	**55**	15	13	11	9	8	7	6	5	4	3	2	1

It's Touching

Fill in the blank boxes with the numbers 1–5. Each full row and column contains the numbers 1, 2, 3, 4, and 5. Each shaded number is the sum of all the numbers touching it.

		4		
	20	1	25	
	3	2	5	
	26	3	24	
	4		2	1

Sudoku

Each row, column, and 3 x 3 box has the digits 1, 2, 3, 4, 5, 6, 7, 8, and 9. Fill in the blanks to complete the puzzle.

3	9	8	7	4	2	1		6
	2	7	6	1	5	3	9	8
1	5	6	8	3	9	4		
9	7			2	6		8	1
2	6		1	5	8		7	3
5	8		3	9			6	4
		2	5	8	3	7	4	9
8	3	5	9	7	4	6	1	
7		9	2	6	1	8	3	5

145   Thinking of a Number

I'm thinking of a four-digit number in which:
- it is divisible by eight.
- it is divisible by nine.
- the first number and the last number are the same.

		9	2

146   Math Path

Pick the best starting number, and then go up/down or left/right until you have touched all of the numbers once. What is the *highest* total you can calculate? Draw your path.

–	12	+	2
4	–	5	–
–	3	–	6
9	+	3	–

Total: _____

147   In Addition

Fill in the blanks with the digits 1–9 so that the sum of each row is the number to the right, and the sum of each column is the number below it.

	8	6		9	28
9	6			5	26
1	2		2	2	9
9		5	7		32
	5	2	8		26
29	29	18	22	23	

Operations Game

148

Directions:

1. Find a partner. Each of you will need a copy of this sheet and a different-colored pen.
2. Look at the rows below. In each row, you have to add, subtract, multiply, and/or divide to get from the first number to the last. The first one has been done for you.
3. Race your partner to solve the rows. You do not have to go in order. The person who solves the most rows wins.
4. Ready, set, go!

| 16 | (+) − / x ÷ | 4 | + − / x (÷) | 5 | (+) − / x ÷ | 5 | + − / x (÷) | 3 | = | 3 |

| 18 | + − / x ÷ | 6 | + − / x ÷ | 6 | + − / x ÷ | 8 | + − / x ÷ | 4 | = | 3 |

| 68 | + − / x ÷ | 34 | + − / x ÷ | 12 | + − / x ÷ | 3 | + − / x ÷ | 6 | = | 44 |

| 6 | + − / x ÷ | 2 | + − / x ÷ | 4 | + − / x ÷ | 18 | + − / x ÷ | 4 | = | 9 |

| 9 | + − / x ÷ | 2 | + − / x ÷ | 6 | + − / x ÷ | 8 | + − / x ÷ | 3 | = | 48 |

| 25 | + − / x ÷ | 5 | + − / x ÷ | 5 | + − / x ÷ | 1 | + − / x ÷ | 5 | = | 20 |

| 11 | + − / x ÷ | 6 | + − / x ÷ | 4 | + − / x ÷ | 7 | + − / x ÷ | 3 | = | 9 |

| 4 | + − / x ÷ | 2 | + − / x ÷ | 13 | + − / x ÷ | 6 | + − / x ÷ | 5 | = | 4 |

| 4 | + − / x ÷ | 8 | + − / x ÷ | 2 | + − / x ÷ | 6 | + − / x ÷ | 3 | = | 10 |

Sudoku
149

Each row, column, and 3 x 3 box has the digits 1, 2, 3, 4, 5, 6, 7, 8, and 9. Fill in the blanks to complete the puzzle.

7	3	2		5	4	1	9	8
5	4	6		8	1		2	
		9	2	7	3	4		5
	6			4		2	8	1
			8	1	2			
1	2	8		3			5	
9		4	1	2	7	5		
	7		3	6		8	4	9
6	5	3	4	9		7	1	2

In Addition
150

Fill in the blanks with the digits 1–9 so that the sum of each row is the number to the right, and the sum of each column is the number below it.

3		2	5	7	**21**
7	6	4			**22**
5	1		3		**17**
		6	8	3	**29**
	4	7		2	**23**
20	**24**	**25**	**25**	**18**	

151 — Thinking of a Number

I'm thinking of a four-digit number in which:
- the first and last digits add up to thirteen.
- the first and second digits multiply to equal eight.
- the third and fourth digits multiply to equal twenty-seven.

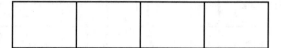

152 — Fill in the Blanks

Fill in the blanks to make this equation true.

$$
\begin{array}{r}
7\ \square\ 9 \\
+\ 5\ \square\ 3\ \square \\
\hline
\square\ 4\ 2\ 6
\end{array}
$$

153 — Addition Tree

Put numbers in the boxes so that all of the boxes add up to the number they came from.

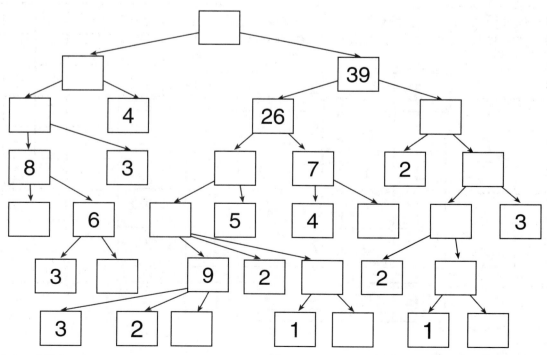

78

Sudoku Challenge

154–157

Each row, column, and 3 x 3 box has the digits 1, 2, 3, 4, 5, 6, 7, 8, and 9.   Fill in the blanks to complete the puzzles.

154

5		6		2	8	3		
	4		6			5	2	
8		9			7		4	6
		7		6	5	2	1	
		4				6		
	6	1	7	4		9		
6	7		1			4		2
	9	2			6		5	
		5	2	7		8		9

155

		2	4				9	3
	7			2		6	8	
5	1			3	6	4		
	3	8		4	5	7		2
7								9
2		6	7	9		1	4	
		5	3	1			7	4
	2	7		8			1	
1	8				7	2		

156

	1		2				9	
	9	8	6	4		1	3	
	6	2		9			5	8
		3	1	7			6	
2	4						1	9
	7			5	2	3		
4	3			1			9	2
	2	1		6	9	5	7	
	5				3		4	

157

7		4	8		5			3
9		2			3		6	8
	1				7	2	4	
8	7		2	9		6		
6								9
		9		3	6		8	2
	8	6	3				9	
4	3		6			8		7
2			1		4	3		6

158 Mike, Anne, Fred, and Kate

Mike, Anne, Fred, and Kate went to different schools. Read each clue. Then, mark the chart with **X**s to see who went to which school.

Clues:

✔ Neither of the boys went to Longfellow or Emerson.

✔ Fred didn't go to Dickinson.

✔ Anne didn't go to Longfellow.

	Longfellow	Dickinson	Whittier	Emerson
Mike				
Anne				
Fred				
Kate				

Answers:

Where did Mike go to school?

_____

Where did Anne go to school?

_____

Where did Fred go to school?

_____

Where did Kate go to school?

_____

159 How Old?

Brian is seven years younger than his older brother.

In two years, his brother will be twice as old as Brian is now.

How old are Brian and his brother? _____

_____

Add One or Two

160

Directions:

1. Find a partner. Each player should use a different-colored pen.
2. Look at the boxes below.
3. Take turns coloring in boxes.
4. You can color in either one or two boxes per turn.
5. Whoever colors in the last box wins.
6. If you have time, play again. This time, whoever colors in the last box loses!

Example:

Game Boards:

1.

2.

3.

4.

5.

6.

7.

8.

What's Next?

161

Draw the shape that should come next.

○ ○ □ △ ○ ○ □ △ ○ ○ □ △ ○ ○ ___

Kara's Kitten

162

Kara lost her kitten. Can you help her find it? Circle the correct kitten.

Here are facts about Kara's kitten:

✔ It is wearing a collar.

✔ It has a short tail.

✔ It has black feet.

Four-in-a-Row

Directions:

1. Find a partner.
2. Choose **X**s or **O**s.
3. Take turns putting an **X** or an **O** in a box.
4. Try to make four in a row, either up-and-down or right-and-left (no diagonals).
5. At the end, count how many four-in-a-rows you made. The person who makes the most wins.
6. If you have time, play again!

Example:

Game Boards:

Letter Box

164

Put the letters A, B, and C in the boxes so that:

- D and A are not in the same row or column.
- A and B are not in the same row.

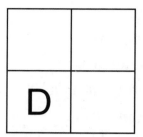

How Old?

165

David is three years older than his brother.

In two years, the sum of their ages will be 19.

How old are David and his brother? _____

_____

Odd Animal Out

166

Circle the animal that doesn't belong.

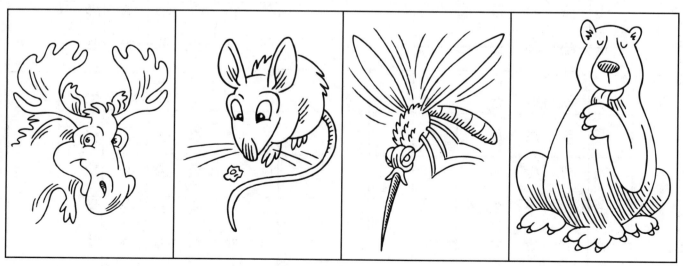

Why doesn't it belong? _____

Pipe Layer

167

Directions:

1. Find a partner.
2. Look at one of the four game boards below. One of you will draw lines connecting black dots, and the other will draw lines connecting white dots. If you are connecting white dots, you are trying to make a path all the way across, from the right to the left. If you are connecting black dots, you are trying to make a path all the way from the top to the bottom.
3. Take turns. You can draw a line connecting dots up-and-down or left-and-right anywhere on the board (between two dots of your color). But, you can't cross your partner's lines!
4. *Hint:* You don't want to get blocked! But, if your partner is getting close, you can draw a line to block him or her.
5. The person who makes it all the way across first wins.
6. If you have time, play again.

Game Boards:

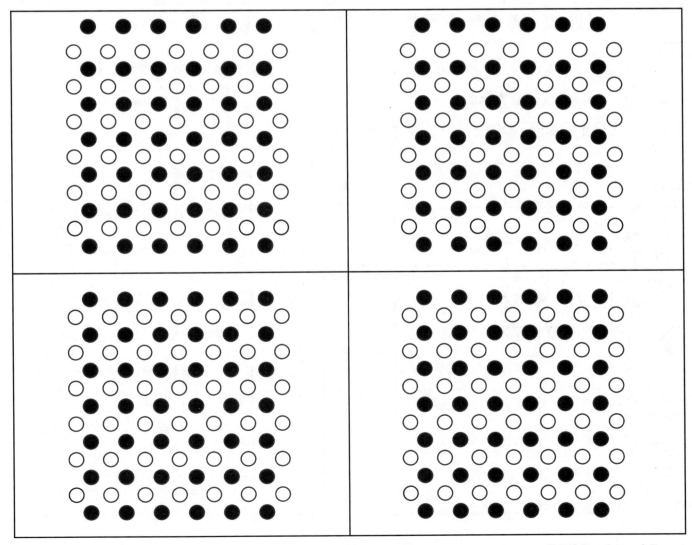

Letter Box

168

Put the letters A, B, D, E, and F in the boxes so that:

- moving clockwise, you could spell the word *fade* (in order).
- F and C are not in the same column.
- B and C are not in the same row.

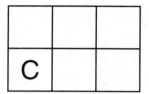

Mike, Anne, Fred, Kate, and Tom

169

Mike, Anne, Fred, Kate, and Tom got up at different times. Read each clue. Then, mark the chart with **X**s to see in which order they woke up.

Clues:

✔ None of the boys got up first or last.

✔ Kate got up before Anne.

✔ Mike got up before Fred, but after Tom.

	First	Second	Third	Fourth	Fifth
Mike					
Anne					
Fred					
Kate					
Tom					

Answers:

When did Mike wake up?

_____

When did Anne wake up?

_____

When did Fred wake up?

_____

When did Kate wake up?

_____

When did Tom wake up?

_____

170   Reversi

Directions:

1. Find a partner and two pencils.
2. One of you is **X**s and the other is **O**s.
3. Take turns marking your letter (**X** or **O**) on the game board.
4. Try to trap your opponent's letter between two of yours. If you trap a letter, it turns into yours—erase your opponent's trapped letter, and replace it with your own.
5. At the end, the person with the most letters on the board wins!
6. If you have time, make your own game board and play again!

Example:

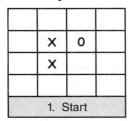 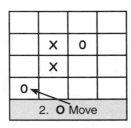 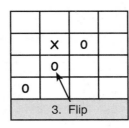 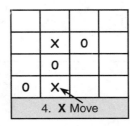 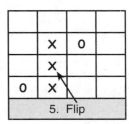

| 1. Start | 2. **O** Move | 3. Flip | 4. **X** Move | 5. Flip |

Game Board:

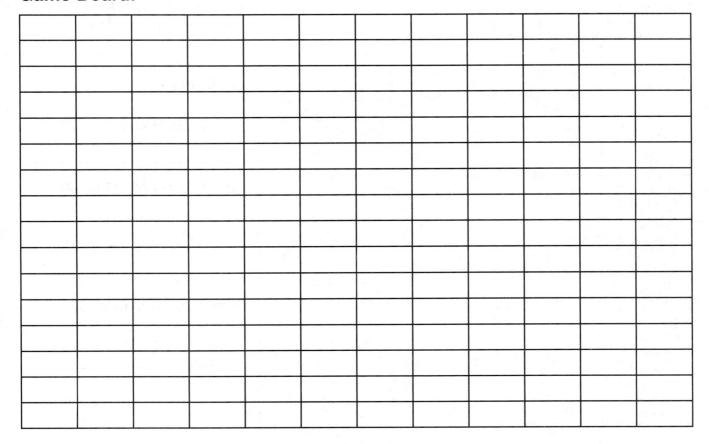

What's Next?

171

Draw the shape that should come next.

$$\bigcirc \triangle \square \bigcirc \bigcirc \triangle \square \bigcirc \bigcirc \bigcirc \triangle \square \bigcirc \bigcirc \bigcirc \underline{\quad}$$

Alice's Book

172

Alice lost her book! Can you help her find it? Circle the correct answer.

Here are facts about Alice's book:

✔ It is thick.

✔ It has a title on the cover.

✔ It does not have a stripe on the spine.

Blocked

Directions:

1. Find a partner and two pencils.

2. Take turns drawing lines from one dot to another. You can only draw vertical lines, and your partner can only draw horizontal lines.

3. Once any line touches a dot, the dot is closed and cannot be used again.

4. The first person who cannot make a move loses.

5. If you have time, play again.

Example:

Game Boards:

Odd Animal Out

174

Circle the animal that doesn't belong.

Why doesn't it belong? _____

Mike, Anne, Fred, Kate, and Tom

175

Mike, Anne, Fred, Kate, and Tom earned different grades on the last math test. Read each clue. Then, mark the chart with **X**s to see who earned which grade.

Clues:

✔ Anne did better than Fred and Kate, but worse than Mike.

✔ Kate didn't earn a B−.

✔ Mike didn't earn an A+.

	A+	A−	B+	B	B−
Mike					
Anne					
Fred					
Kate					
Tom					

Answers:

Which grade did Mike earn?

_____

Which grade did Anne earn?

_____

Which grade did Fred earn?

_____

Which grade did Kate earn?

_____

Which grade did Tom earn?

_____

90

Boxed Out

176

Directions:

1. Find a partner. Each player should use a different-colored pen.
2. Look at the dots below.
3. Take turns drawing a short line between two dots.
4. Try to make closed boxes. When you make a box, color it in. Then, go again.
5. The person who makes the most boxes wins.

Example:

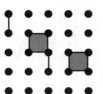

Game Board:

177 What's Next?

Draw the shape that should come next.

□○△○○□△○○□△○○□△○○□△○○□ ____

178 Tanya's Balloon

Tanya lost her balloon! Can you help her find it? Circle the correct answer.

Here are facts about Tanya's balloon:

✔ It has a string. ✔ It has a star on it. ✔ The balloon's shape is colored in.	  

  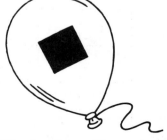

92

Ship Shapes
179

Directions:

1. Find a partner. You will each need two copies of the game board below.
2. On one of your game boards, color in the following "ships." You can mark them up-and-down or left-and-right (vertically or horizontally). Don't show your partner!

Aircraft Carrier:

Battleship:

Cruiser:

Patrol Boat:

Submarine:

3. Take turns trying to find each other's ships. For example, you might say "A8" and your partner would say "hit" or "miss." Mark your guesses on your game board. Mark your partner's guesses on the game board with your ships. Hide your game boards while you are playing!
4. Once your partner has hit every space of one of your ships, it is sunk.
5. The first person to sink all of the other's ships wins.

Game Board:

	1	2	3	4	5	6	7	8	9	10
A										
B										
C										
D										
E										
F										
G										
H										
I										
J										

Letter Box

180

Put the letters A, C, D, F, G, H, and I in the boxes so that:

- A, B, or C are not in the same row or column.
- E, F, or G are not in the same row or column.
- A and G are not in the same row.
- A and E are in the same column.
- C and G are in the same column.
- D and F are in the same column.
- H and G are in the same column.

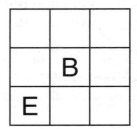

Mike, Anne, and Fred

181

Mike, Anne, and Fred ate snacks and played sports. Read each clue. Then, mark the chart with **X**s to see who ate which snack and played which sport.

Clues:

✔ The person who played tennis ate an apple.

✔ Anne didn't eat an apple or a PB & J sandwich. She also didn't play hockey.

✔ Mike didn't eat a PB & J sandwich.

	Pizza	Apple	PB & J	Soccer	Tennis	Hockey
Mike						
Anne						
Fred						

Answers:

What snack did Mike eat?

What sport did he play?

_____

What snack did Anne eat?

What sport did she play?

_____

What snack did Fred eat?

What sport did he play?

_____

Four-in-a-Line

182

Directions:

1. Find a partner. One of you is **X**s and the other is **O**s.

2. Look at the game boards below. Imagine you could drop an **X** or an **O** into the top of one of the game boards,\ and it would fall down to the bottom.

3. Take turns "dropping" your letter. Mark your moves on the game board.

4. The first person to make four in a row wins.

5. If you have time, play again.

Game Boards:

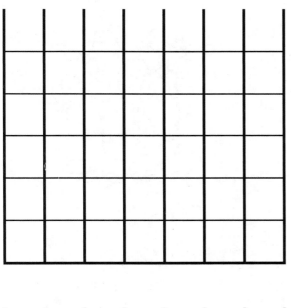

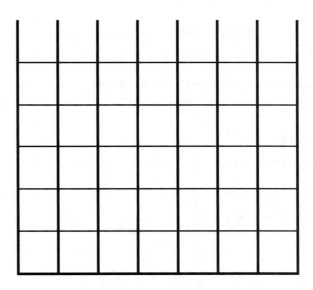

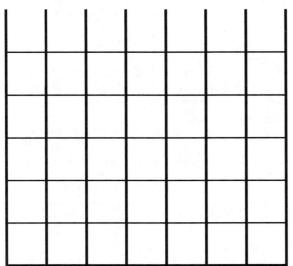

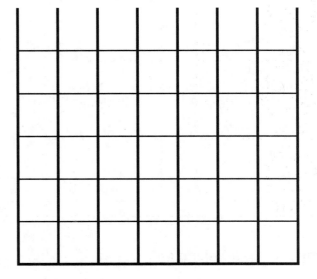

What's Next?

183

Draw the shape that should come next.

O▢△O O▢△O▢△O O▢△O▢△O O▢△O▢△O O ___

How Old?

184

The sum of Matt's age and his brother's is twenty-one.

In five years, Matt will be five years younger than his brother is at that time.

How old are Matt and his brother? _____

_____

Odd Animal Out

185

Circle the animal that doesn't belong.

Why doesn't it belong? _____

Sprouts

Directions:

1. Find a partner. This game is tricky, so read the directions carefully!

2. Start with three dots on a piece of paper (like those given below).

3. Take turns moving. Each move has two parts:

   A. Draw a line connecting two dots (or a dot to itself). This line cannot cross any other line. No dot can have more than three lines coming out of it.

   B. Draw one new dot anywhere on your new line.

4. The winner is the last person who can make a move. Remember, once a dot has three lines coming out of it, it is blocked.

   Here is how a game might start:

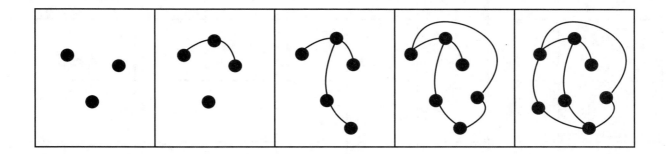

Mike, Anne, Fred, and Kate

187

Mike, Anne, Fred, and Kate ran a race while wearing different-colored shirts. Read each clue. Then, mark the chart with **X**s to see where each kid finished in the race and which shirt he or she wore.

Clues:

✔ Neither of the boys finished first or last.

✔ Neither the person wearing yellow nor the person wearing green finished first or second.

✔ Anne didn't finish fourth, and she didn't wear blue.

✔ Mike finished ahead of Fred.

✔ Fred didn't wear green.

	Green	Blue	Red	Yellow	First	Second	Third	Fourth
Mike								
Anne								
Fred								
Kate								

Answers:

What color did Mike wear? How did he finish?

_____

What color did Anne wear? How did she finish?

_____

What color did Fred wear? How did he finish?

_____

What color did Kate wear? How did she finish?

_____

Letter Box

188

Put the letters A, C, D, E, G, H, and I in the boxes so that:

- one row reads D, E, H.
- C, G, and E are in the same column.
- B, C, and I are in the same row.

F		
		B

How Old?

189

Adam has a brother and a sister.

His brother is five years older than his sister, and she is three years older than Adam.

The sum of their ages is 38.

How old are the three kids? _____

_____

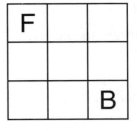

Odd Animal Out

190

Circle the animal that doesn't belong.

Why doesn't it belong? _____

Answer Key

Note: Answers are organized according to puzzle number, not page number.

Picture Puzzles

1. ten

2. Answer may be rotated.

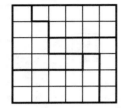

4. Answer may be rotated.

5. In the second picture, the sphinx has a nose, beard, and no tail. It also has an extra toe on its back foot, is wearing a headband, and has an extra front leg. In addition, the pyramid is missing.

6.

Ad Number	What Is It?
3	Pure White Rock Potash (soap)
1	Buckskin Glue
4	Harrison's Flavoring Extracts
2	Unicorn Drops (cough drops)

8.

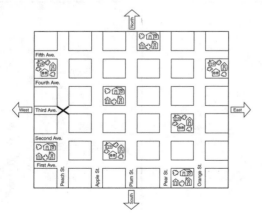

9.

10. ill in bed
    excuse me
    too little, too late
    just between you and me

12.

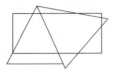

13. Answer may be rotated.

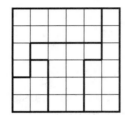

14. Answer may be rotated.

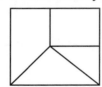

15. In the second picture, the girl's hair is curly, not straight. Also, the girl is wearing a bracelet but is not wearing shoes. In addition, she is wearing a v-neck shirt, and her eyes are open.

16.

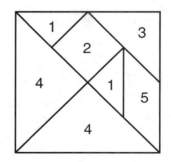

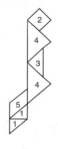

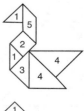

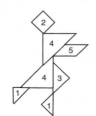

Answer Key (cont.)

17.

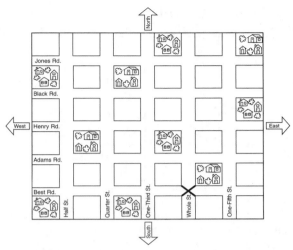

18. too funny for words
banana split

19. eight

20. In the second picture, the boy has sandals on and longer hair. He is not smiling. His swim trunks have stars on them instead of dots. He is also wearing a watch.

22.

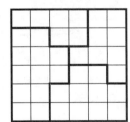

23. Answer may be rotated.

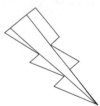

24. Answer may be rotated.

25. twenty-one

26. once upon a time
settle down

27.

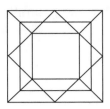

29. small talk
I understand.

30. In the second picture, one black checker is missing, while a white checker has been doubled as a king. One black checker has been replaced with a white one. There is also a full border around the board, and one black square is now white.

32.

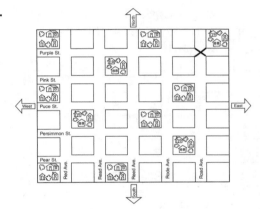

33. Answer may be rotated.

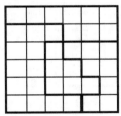

34. Robin Hood
once in my life
Ring Around the Rosie
white out

Word Puzzles

36. Answers will vary but may be similar to:

s	a	y	s
d	**a**	**y**	**s**
d	**a**	**d**	**s**
d	u	d	s

Answer Key *(cont.)*

37. almost, lollipop, oil, little, spill, limitless, low and owl

38.

¹m	²a	³t	⁴e
⁵i	c	o	n
⁶s	e	n	d
⁷o	d	e	s

39. Wait until the (pan darkens) (to add) sauce or (risk unknown) results.

40. a pelican

41. meat, tame, team, mate

42. STEP

44. The (sumo thundered) in, trying to (smother his (mother's) opponent.

45. his homework

46. Answers will vary but may be similar to:

p	i	g	s
p	**i**	**e**	**s**
t	**i**	**e**	**s**
t	o	e	s

47. colds, scold, clods

48. Answers will vary but may be similar to:

m	i	s	t
m	**a**	**s**	**t**
l	**a**	**s**	**t**
l	a	s	h

49. paper, proper, appear, pretty, propose, ump and pump

50.

		O		F			
		R		M	A	N	T	A
		A		U			N
		N		N			T
		G	I	R	A	F	F	E
		U					A
		T					T
M	A	C	A	W			E
		N		T	I	G	E	R

Other words will vary.

51. last, salt, slat

52.

¹s	²n	³o	⁴b
⁵p	o	r	e
⁶u	s	e	s
⁷r	e	s	t

53. GOAT

54. a hot air baboon

55. My am(igo ate m(icrowaved chili on) toast.

56. earth, heart

57. THUMB

58. Order may vary.

   mitten→nail→lighthouse→
   eagle→elephant→thermometer→
   rain→needle→elf

59. Come watch Harmoni(ca Me) fulfi(ll ama)teur dreams.

60.

¹v	²e	³i	⁴n
⁵a	c	r	e
⁶s	h	o	t
⁷t	o	n	s

61. eject, left, energetic, eel and Lee, we and ewe, felt and fleet

62. AIR

63. shout, south

64. The tr(apeze bra)t)s(cowl)ed while arre(sting Ray)

65. fish and ships

67. "Isn't baseba(ll ama)zing?" asked (Ca)therine, her corn(ea gl)eaming.

68. bubble, baseball, abbreviation, hobby, hubbub, absorb, bend

Answer Key *(cont.)*

69. Answers will vary but may be similar to:

s	t	o	p
s	**t**	**o**	**w**
s	**h**	**o**	**w**
c	h	o	w

70.

¹ s	² p	³ u	⁴ n
⁵ c	o	n	e
⁶ a	l	i	t
⁷ r	o	t	s

71. rates, stare, tears

72. EYE

73. Answers will vary but may include:
    resting, rests, assisting, assign,
    assists, coasting, coasts, coach, coats,
    rusting, rusts, ruts, trusting, trusts,
    truck, trumpet, truth, listing, lists, lick,
    disgusting, disguise, disgusts, crusting,
    cruise, crusts, crumpet, boasting,
    boasts, boats, promise

74. electricity (*Hint:* Code is +2, −1, +2,
    +1, etc.)

75. The ⟨crowds⟩ ab⟨hor⟩ sel⟨fish⟩ ⟨AM⟩ stereo
    use.

76. Answers will vary but may be similar to:

s	p	i	n
s	**p**	**i**	**t**
s	**p**	**o**	**t**
s	**l**	**o**	**t**
p	l	o	t

77. FOOT

78.

¹ p	² l	³ o	⁴ w
⁵ l	i	n	e
⁶ o	v	e	n
⁷ t	e	s	t

79. add and dad, do and odd, did, dud,
    added, granddaddy, wedding

80. The missing planet is Earth.

				J					
			U	R	A	N	U	S	·
			P			E			
			I		P	L	U	T	O
			T			T			
		M	E	R	C	U	R	Y	
			R			N			
					V	E	N	U	S
								A	
								T	
								U	
							M	A	R	S
								N	

   Other words will vary.

81. Is the ye⟨ti⟩ Ger⟨man⟩, or is ⟨Cat⟩herine
    ⟨gull⟩ible?

82. acre, care, race

83. oicurmt ("Oh, I see you are empty.")

84. flu and fluff, after, effort, affect, fact

85. Answers will vary but may be similar to:

s	c	o	l	d
s	**c**	**a**	**l**	**d**
s	**c**	**a**	**l**	**e**
s	**c**	**a**	**r**	**e**
s	h	a	r	e

86. straw, warts

87.

¹ c	² l	³ u	⁴ b
⁵ l	a	n	e
⁶ a	c	i	d
⁷ p	e	t	s

Answer Key (cont.)

89. pals, slap, Alps, laps

90. juggle, grudge, age, egg, giggling, zigzagging, goggles

91. The overcrowded wheelbarrow led to a difficult size brawl.

92. EGG

93. Answers will vary but may be similar to:

g	i	r	l	s
g	**i**	**l**	**l**	**s**
p	**i**	**l**	**l**	**s**
p	**i**	**l**	**e**	**s**
p	o	l	e	s

94. coats, tacos, coast

95.

¹ s	² o	³ f	⁴ t
⁵ k	n	e	e
⁶ i	c	e	s
⁷ m	e	l	t

96. least, tales, steal, slate

97. "The slob's terrified to hang up pylons!" said his mother.

98. fates, feast, feats

99. ARM

Number Puzzles

100.

4	2	1	3
1	**3**	4	**2**
3	4	**2**	1
2	1	3	**4**

101.

4	7	8	6	25
4	**5**	2	3	14
3	2	5	2	12
2	**3**	9	8	22
13	17	24	19	

102.

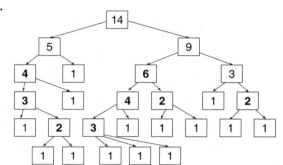

103.

4	1	5	**3**	**2**
1	26	**3**	23	3
3	**5**	4	2	1
5	25	2	23	4
2	3	1	4	**5**

104. Answers will vary but may be similar to:

48	÷	2	+	14	+	8	x	3
−	3	+	20	+	1	+	3	x
24	÷	8	x	8	x	3	x	6
−	14	−	8	x	12	−	2	+
18	+	1	+	1	+	4	x	6
x	6	+	9	+	14	+	9	+
4	+	17	+	8	−	4	+	8
−	2	x	12	+	2	+	6	+
2	+	2	−	10	x	4	x	4

105. 10

Paths will vary but may be similar to:

6	+	5
+	3	−
2	−	4

Answer Key *(cont.)*

106.

4	3	1	2
1	2	4	3
2	4	3	1
3	1	2	4

107.

```
  1  4  4
+ 4  7  3
---------
  6  1  7
```

108.

4	5	6	3

109.

2	9	5	7	23
3	6	1	4	14
6	3	2	9	20
5	9	7	2	23

16	27	15	22

110.

325 − 172	228 + 449	21 x 8	153 ÷ 17	812 + 94	19 x 8
153	677	168	9	906	152
14 x 19	240 ÷ 15	164 − 87	634 + 436	322 ÷ 23	24 x 28
266	16	77	1070	14	672
150 ÷ 3	472 + 598	243 ÷ 9	32 x 35	756 − 348	13 x 13
50	1070	27	1120	408	169

6 x 16	4 x 14	9 x 19	342 ÷ 38	674 + 249	783 ÷ 29
96	56	171	9	923	27
2 x 12	598 ÷ 26	8 x 18	72 − 34	34 + 17	4 x 9
24	23	144	38	51	36
7 x 17	3 x 13	5 x 15	27 x 31	15 x 18	18 x 26
119	39	75	837	270	468

111.

2	4	1	3
1	3	2	4
4	2	3	1
3	1	4	2

112.

4	6	8	4	22
2	7	2	8	19
7	9	3	4	23
6	7	3	9	25

19	29	16	25

113.

```
  2  7  9
+ 2  4  9
---------
  5  2  8
```

114. 7

Paths will vary but may be similar to:

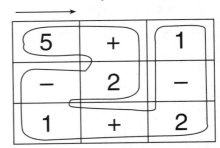

115.

4	1	3	2	5
2	22	1	20	3
5	4	2	3	1
1	28	4	22	4
3	4	5	1	2

Answer Key *(cont.)*

116.

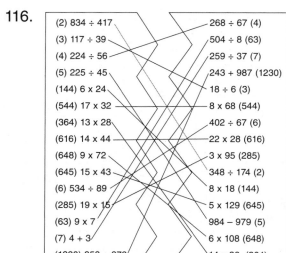

(2) 834 ÷ 417   268 ÷ 67 (4)
(3) 117 ÷ 39   504 ÷ 8 (63)
(4) 224 ÷ 56   259 ÷ 37 (7)
(5) 225 ÷ 45   243 + 987 (1230)
(144) 6 x 24   18 ÷ 6 (3)
(544) 17 x 32   8 x 68 (544)
(364) 13 x 28   402 ÷ 67 (6)
(616) 14 x 44   22 x 28 (616)
(648) 9 x 72   3 x 95 (285)
(645) 15 x 43   348 ÷ 174 (2)
(6) 534 ÷ 89   8 x 18 (144)
(285) 19 x 15   5 x 129 (645)
(63) 9 x 7   984 – 979 (5)
(7) 4 + 3   6 x 108 (648)
(1230) 358 + 872   14 x 26 (364)

117.

2	1	4	**3**
4	**3**	**1**	2
1	**2**	**3**	4
3	4	2	**1**

118.

8	**7**	**6**	**5**

119.

```
                    25
            14              11
        13      1       8       3
      12    1        6   2    1   2
     1   11      5   1  1   1  1   1
       6  5    1  1  3
```

120.

```
      8   6   5
  +   6   9   7
  -----------------
    1   5   6   2
```

121. 6

Paths will vary but may be similar to:

16	+	5
–	9	–
8	–	12

122.

7	4	**3**	1		15
5	**1**	9	6		21
2	6	**3**	**4**		15
1	5	2	**2**		10

15	16	17	13

123.

16	⊕ or –	3	+ or ⊖	9	⊕ or –	5	=	15
67	+ or ⊖	22	⊕ or –	9	+ or ⊖	34	=	20
82	⊕ or –	13	+ or ⊖	67	⊕ or –	19	=	47
18	⊕ or –	76	+ or ⊖	47	+ or ⊖	19	=	28
44	+ or ⊖	36	+ or ⊖	7	⊕ or –	98	=	99
57	+ or ⊖	17	+ or ⊖	23	⊕ or –	76	=	93
40	+ or ⊖	13	⊕ or –	12	⊕ or –	14	=	53
76	+ or ⊖	57	+ or ⊖	9	⊕ or –	87	=	97

124.

3	**4**	**5**	**6**

125.

1	**3**	2	**5**	4
2	17	**1**	25	3
4	1	3	2	**5**
5	26	4	26	1
3	1	**5**	**4**	2

Answer Key *(cont.)*

126.

3	6	5	1	2	4
4	1	2	5	3	6
2	3	4	6	5	1
6	5	1	2	4	3
1	2	3	4	6	5
5	4	6	3	1	2

127.

6	1	1	7	15
7	3	1	1	12
3	9	7	1	20
8	6	5	2	21

24	19	14	11

128.

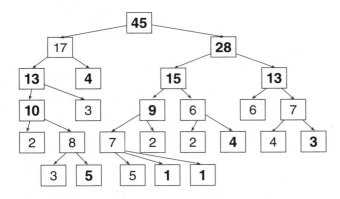

129. Answers will vary but may be similar to:

Player #1		Player #2
1 ②3④5⑥⑦8⑨⑪⑬	**52**	⑬⑪⑨8⑦7 6 5④3 2 1
1 2 3 4 ⑤6⑦8 9⑪⑬	**45**	13⑪⑨8⑦7 6 5④③②①
①2 3 4 5 6⑦⑧⑨⑪⑬	**49**	13⑪⑨8⑦7 6⑤④③②1
①2 3 4 5 6⑦8 9⑪⑬	**32**	13⑪⑨8⑦7 6 5④3 2 1
1 2 3④5⑥⑦⑧⑨⑪⑬	**63**	⑬⑪⑨⑧⑦7 6⑤④③②①
1②3 4 5 6⑦8⑨⑪⑬	**56**	⑬⑪⑨8⑦7⑥⑤4③②①
1 2 3 4 5⑥7 8 9 11⑬	**19**	13⑪⑨8⑦7 6 5 4 3 2 1
①2 3 4 5⑥⑦8⑨⑪⑬	**47**	⑬⑪⑨8⑦7 6 5④3②①
1 2 3④5⑥⑦⑧⑨⑪⑬	**58**	13⑪⑨⑧⑦7 6⑤4③②①
1②3④5⑥⑦⑧⑨⑪⑬	**60**	⑬⑪⑨8⑦7 6⑤④③②①
1 2 3 4 5 6⑦8⑨⑪⑬	**40**	13⑪⑨8⑦⑥5④3②①

130.

$$\begin{array}{ccc}
 & \boxed{9}\ \boxed{4}\ 6 \\
+ & \boxed{5}\ 5\ 2\ \boxed{8} \\
\hline
 & 6\ 4\ 7\ 4
\end{array}$$

131.

1	6	3	2	4	5
4	5	2	1	6	3
2	1	4	3	5	6
6	3	5	4	1	2
5	2	1	6	3	4
3	4	6	5	2	1

132.

4	9	3	9	25
1	5	4	7	17
2	2	5	3	12
3	4	2	6	15

10	20	14	25

133.

5	4	2	3	1
3	25	1	21	5
1	5	4	3	2
4	25	3	27	3
2	1	5	3	4

134.

8	8	8	8

135. 26

Paths will vary but may be
similar to:

18	–	1
–	22	–
7	+	6

Answer Key *(cont.)*

136. Answers will vary but may be similar to:

16	+	8	+	8	− 5	x 4
x	34	− 2	+	27	+ 3	+
3	−	8	+ 2	+	2	x 12
−	8	−	34	+ 4	+ 5	−
16	+	12	+	28	− 4	− 6
+	4	x	30	− 20	x 13	+
18	− 2	÷	2	+	4	x 2
+	2	+	2	x 16	x 16	+
12	x	8	+	30	+ 2	+ 14

137.

1	2	5	4	6	3
6	4	3	5	2	1
5	3	1	2	4	6
2	6	4	3	1	5
3	1	2	6	5	4
4	5	6	1	3	2

138.

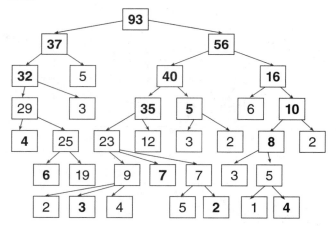

139.

```
    5  6  5
 +  3  7  6  6
    4  3  3  1
```

140.

3	4	6	8

141.

7	4	1	4	16
3	5	6	2	16
2	8	9	9	28
2	8	1	5	16

14	25	17	20

142. Answers will vary but may be similar to:

Player #1		Player #2
① 2 3 4 5 6 ⑦ 8 ⑨ ⑪ 13 ⑮	56	15 ⑬ ⑪ ⑨ 8 ⑦ 6 ⑤ 4 3 ② ①
1 2 ③ 4 ⑤ 6 ⑦ 8 9 ⑪ ⑬ ⑮	63	⑮ 13 ⑪ ⑨ 8 7 ⑥ ⑤ ④ ③ ② ①
① 2 3 4 5 6 7 8 9 11 ⑬ ⑮	38	⑮ 13 11 9 ⑧ ⑦ 6 ⑤ 4 ③ ② 1
1 2 ③ 4 5 ⑥ ⑦ ⑧ 9 ⑪ 13 15	44	⑮ ⑬ ⑪ 9 8 7 6 ⑤ 4 3 2 1
1 ② 3 4 5 ⑥ ⑦ ⑧ ⑨ ⑪ 13 ⑮	71	⑮ ⑬ ⑪ ⑨ 8 7 ⑥ ⑤ 4 ③ ② 1
1 2 3 4 5 6 7 ⑧ 9 ⑪ 13 ⑮	47	15 ⑬ ⑪ ⑨ ⑧ 7 ⑥ 5 4 3 2 1
1 ② 3 4 ⑤ 6 ⑦ 8 9 ⑪ 13 15	53	15 ⑬ ⑪ ⑨ ⑧ 7 ⑥ 5 ④ 3 2 1
1 2 3 ④ 5 6 7 8 9 11 13 ⑮	19	15 ⑬ 11 9 8 ⑦ 6 ⑤ 4 3 2 1
1 2 3 4 5 6 7 ⑧ 9 11 ⑬ ⑮	36	15 ⑬ ⑪ 9 ⑧ 7 6 ⑤ 4 3 2 1
1 ② 3 4 5 6 7 8 ⑨ ⑪ ⑬ ⑮	50	15 13 ⑪ ⑨ ⑧ ⑦ 6 ⑤ 4 ③ ② 1
1 2 3 4 5 ⑥ ⑦ ⑧ ⑨ ⑪ ⑬ ⑮	69	⑮ ⑬ ⑪ ⑨ ⑧ 7 6 ⑤ ④ ③ 2 1
1 2 3 4 5 ⑥ 7 ⑧ ⑨ ⑪ ⑬ 15	62	⑮ ⑬ ⑪ ⑨ ⑧ 7 6 ⑤ 4 3 2 ①
1 ② 3 4 ⑤ 6 7 8 ⑨ ⑪ ⑬ ⑮	55	15 13 ⑪ ⑨ ⑧ ⑦ ⑥ ⑤ ④ ③ ② 1

143.

2	3	4	1	5
4	20	1	25	3
1	3	2	5	4
5	26	3	24	2
3	4	5	2	1

144.

3	9	8	7	4	2	1	5	6
4	2	7	6	1	5	3	9	8
1	5	6	8	3	9	4	2	7
9	7	3	4	2	6	5	8	1
2	6	4	1	5	8	9	7	3
5	8	1	3	9	7	2	6	4
6	1	2	5	8	3	7	4	9
8	3	5	9	7	4	6	1	2
7	4	9	2	6	1	8	3	5

145.

2	5	9	2

146. 10

Paths will vary but may be similar to:

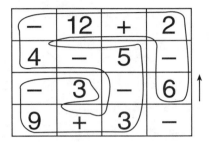

−	12	+	2
4	−	5	−
−	3	−	6
9	+	3	−

147.

3	8	6	2	9	**28**
9	6	3	3	5	**26**
1	2	2	2	2	**9**
9	8	5	7	3	**32**
7	5	2	8	4	**26**
29	**29**	**18**	**22**	**23**	

148.

- 16 ⊕ 4 ÷ 5 ⊕ 5 ÷ 3 = 3
- 18 ⊕ 6 ÷ 6 ⊕ 8 ÷ 4 = 3
- 68 ⊕ 34 ⊕ 12 − 3 ⊕ 6 = 44
- 6 ⊕ 2 + 4 ⊗ 18 ÷ 4 = 9
- 9 + 2 ⊕ 6 ⊖ 8 + 3 = 48
- 25 ⊗ 5 ÷ 5 ⊗ 1 ⊖ 5 = 20
- 11 ⊖ 6 ⊗ 4 ⊕ 7 ÷ 3 = 9
- 4 + 2 ⊗ 13 ⊖ 6 ÷ 5 = 4
- 4 ⊕ 8 ⊗ 2 ⊕ 6 ÷ 3 = 10

(Each operator box shows the choices + − over × ÷; the circled operator is the answer.)

149.

7	3	2	**6**	5	4	1	9	8
5	4	6	**9**	8	1	**3**	2	**7**
8	**1**	9	2	7	3	4	**6**	5
3	6	**7**	**5**	4	**9**	2	8	1
4	**9**	**5**	8	1	2	**6**	**7**	**3**
1	2	8	**7**	3	**6**	**9**	5	**4**
9	**8**	4	1	2	7	5	**3**	**6**
2	7	**1**	3	6	**5**	8	4	9
6	5	3	4	9	**8**	7	1	2

150.

3	**4**	2	5	7	**21**
7	6	4	**1**	**4**	**22**
5	1	**6**	3	**2**	**17**
3	**9**	6	8	3	**29**
2	4	7	**8**	2	**23**
20	**24**	**25**	**25**	**18**	

151.

4	2	3	9

152.

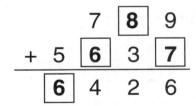

```
    7  [8]  9
+ 5 [6]  3 [7]
[6]  4   2  6
```

153.

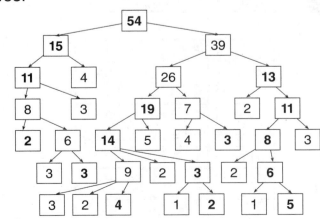

Answer Key *(cont.)*

154.

5	1	6	4	2	8	3	9	7
7	4	3	6	9	1	5	2	8
8	2	9	5	3	7	1	4	6
3	8	7	9	6	5	2	1	4
9	5	4	8	1	2	6	7	3
2	6	1	7	4	3	9	8	5
6	7	8	1	5	9	4	3	2
4	9	2	3	8	6	7	5	1
1	3	5	2	7	4	8	6	9

155.

8	6	2	4	7	1	5	9	3
4	7	3	5	2	9	6	8	1
5	1	9	8	3	6	4	2	7
9	3	8	1	4	5	7	6	2
7	4	1	2	6	8	3	5	9
2	5	6	7	9	3	1	4	8
6	9	5	3	1	2	8	7	4
3	2	7	6	8	4	9	1	5
1	8	4	9	5	7	2	3	6

156.

3	1	4	2	8	5	6	9	7
5	9	8	6	4	7	1	3	2
7	6	2	3	9	1	4	5	8
9	8	3	1	7	4	2	6	5
2	4	5	8	3	6	7	1	9
1	7	6	9	5	2	3	8	4
4	3	7	5	1	8	9	2	6
8	2	1	4	6	9	5	7	3
6	5	9	7	2	3	8	4	1

157.

7	6	4	8	2	5	9	1	3
9	5	2	4	1	3	7	6	8
3	1	8	9	6	7	2	4	5
8	7	5	2	9	1	6	3	4
6	2	3	5	4	8	1	7	9
1	4	9	7	3	6	5	8	2
5	8	6	3	7	2	4	9	1
4	3	1	6	5	9	8	2	7
2	9	7	1	8	4	3	5	6

Logic Puzzles

158.

	Longfellow	Dickinson	Whittier	Emerson
Mike				
Anne				
Fred				
Kate				

Where did Mike go to school? __Dickinson__

Where did Anne go to school? __Emerson__

Where did Fred go to school? __Whittier__

Where did Kate go to school? __Longfellow__

159. Brian is nine and his older brother is sixteen.

161.

162. Kara's kitten has a short tail, black feet, and a collar.

164.

C	A
D	B

165. David is nine and his brother is six.

166. The bear does not belong because it doesn't start with an "m." Or, the mosquito does not belong because it is not a mammal, and it is the only animal with wings.

168.

B	F	A
C	E	D

Answer Key (cont.)

169.

	First	Second	Third	Fourth	Fifth
Mike	X	X		X	X
Anne	X	X	X	X	
Fred	X	X	X		X
Kate		X	X	X	X
Tom	X		X	X	X

When did Mike wake up? _____third_____

When did Anne wake up? _____fifth_____

When did Fred wake up? _____fourth_____

When did Kate wake up? _____first_____

When did Tom wake up? _____second_____

171.

172. Alice's book is thick with a title on the cover.

Adventure ISLAND

174. The seagull does not belong because it doesn't swim in the ocean, and it has feathers and a beak.

175.

	A+	A−	B+	B	B−
Mike	X		X	X	X
Anne	X	X		X	X
Fred	X	X	X	X	
Kate	X	X	X		X
Tom		X	X	X	X

Which grade did Mike earn? _____A−_____

Which grade did Anne earn? _____B+_____

Which grade did Fred earn? _____B−_____

Which grade did Kate earn? _____B_____

Which grade did Tom earn? _____A+_____

177.

178. Tanya's balloon has a colored-in star on it. It also has a string.

180.

A	F	H
I	B	G
E	D	C

181.

	Pizza	Apple	PB & J	Soccer	Tennis	Hockey
Mike	X		X	X		X
Anne		X	X		X	X
Fred	X	X		X	X	

What snack did Mike eat? What sport did he play?
Mike ate an apple and played tennis.

What snack did Anne eat? What sport did she play?
Anne ate pizza and played soccer.

What snack did Fred eat? What sport did he play?
Fred ate a PB & J sandwich and played hockey.

183.

184. Matt is eight and his brother is thirteen.

185. The beetle does not belong because it is the only animal with six legs.

Answer Key (cont.)

187.

	Green	Blue	Red	Yellow	First	Second	Third	Fourth
Mike	✕		✕	✕	✕		✕	✕
Anne	✕	✕		✕		✕	✕	✕
Fred	✕	✕	✕		✕	✕		✕
Kate		✕	✕	✕	✕	✕	✕	

What color did Mike wear? How did he finish?
<u>Mike wore blue and finished second.</u>

What color did Anne wear? How did she finish?
<u>Anne wore red and finished first.</u>

What color did Fred wear? How did he finish?
<u>Fred wore yellow and finished third.</u>

What color did Kate wear? How did she finish?
<u>Kate wore green and finished fourth.</u>

188.

F	G	A
D	E	H
I	C	B

189. Adam is nine, his sister is twelve, and his brother is seventeen.

190. The salamander does not belong because it is the only animal whose primary mode of movement is not jumping. Or, the kangaroo does not belong because it is a warm-blooded animal.